I SAW A PILLAR OF LIGHT

*Sacred, Saving Truths
from Joseph Smith's First Vision*

Also by Robert L. Millet

The Holy Spirit	*Talking with God*
The Atoning One	*Men of Influence*
Whatever Happened to Faith?	*Holding Fast*
Precept upon Precept	*Men of Valor*
Men of Covenant	*What Happened to the Cross?*
Living in the Millennium	*Are We There Yet?*
Living in the Eleventh Hour	*Getting at the Truth*
Lehi's Dream	*Grace Works*
Making Sense of the Book of Revelation	*When a Child Wanders*

I SAW A PILLAR OF
LIGHT

*Sacred, Saving Truths
from Joseph Smith's First Vision*

ROBERT L. MILLET

DESERET
BOOK

Salt Lake City, Utah

© 2020 Robert L. Millet

All rights reserved. No part of this book may be reproduced in any form or by any means without permission in writing from the publisher, Deseret Book Company, at permissions@deseretbook.com or PO Box 30178, Salt Lake City, Utah 84130. This work is not an official publication of The Church of Jesus Christ of Latter-day Saints. The views expressed herein are the responsibility of the author and do not necessarily represent the position of the Church or of Deseret Book Company.

DESERET BOOK is a registered trademark of Deseret Book Company.

Visit us at deseretbook.com

Library of Congress Cataloging-in-Publication Data

Names: Millet, Robert L., author.

Title: I saw a pillar of light : sacred, saving truths from Joseph Smith's First Vision / Robert L. Millet.

Description: Salt Lake City, Utah : Deseret Book, [2020] | Includes bibliographical references and index. | Summary: "Noted Latter-day Saint scholar Robert L. Millet explores the doctrinal and theological implications of the Prophet Joseph Smith's First Vision"—Provided by publisher.

Identifiers: LCCN 2020015352 | ISBN 9781629727998 (hardback)

Subjects: LCSH: Smith, Joseph, Jr., 1805–1844—First Vision. | The Church of Jesus Christ of Latter-day Saints—Doctrines. | The Church of Jesus Christ of Latter-day Saints—History—19th century. | Mormon Church—Doctrines. | Mormon Church—History—19th century. | New York (State)—Church history—19th century.

Classification: LCC BX8695.S6 M55 2020 | DDC 230/.93—dc23

LC record available at https://lccn.loc.gov/2020015352

Printed in the United States of America
PubLitho, Draper, UT

10   9   8   7   6   5   4   3   2   1

"The appearing of the Father and the Son to Joseph Smith is the foundation of this Church. Therein lies the secret of its strength and vitality. This is true, and I bear witness to it. That one revelation answers all the queries of science regarding God and his divine personality. Don't you see what that means? What God is, is answered. His relation to his children is clear. His interest in humanity through authority delegated to man is apparent. The future of the work is assured. These and other glorious truths are clarified by that glorious first vision."
—David O. McKay

"When God the Father and his Son Jesus Christ come to earth, as they did in 1820 when they appeared to the young boy prophet, Joseph Smith, it is not something that concerns only a handful of people. It is a message and a revelation intended for all of our Father's children living upon the face of the earth. It was the greatest event that ever happened in this world since the resurrection of the Master. Sometimes I think we are so close to it that we don't fully appreciate its significance and importance and the magnitude of it. The first vision of the Prophet Joseph Smith is bedrock theology in the Church."
—Ezra Taft Benson

"Actually, the fact that the Father and the Son appeared to an untitled youth is one of the most remarkable aspects of the Restoration. Joseph Smith did not have to 'unlearn' anything. He was tutored personally by Them. Joseph was also tutored by other heavenly messengers. . . . [His] mission in mortality was foreordained. His receptive and pristine mind was open to the Lord's instruction. But, by worldly standards, Joseph was most unlikely. And his task to be the Prophet of this last dispensation seemed totally impossible. . . . This pattern is one the Lord has used repeatedly throughout history."

—Russell M. Nelson

CONTENTS

Preface ix

1. How It All Began 1
2. The Winds of Revivalism 11
3. Entering the Grove 26
4. The Appearance 40
5. "Their Hearts Are Far from Me" 56
6. "All Their Creeds" 74
7. After the Vision 84
8. What Joseph Learned 98
9. Formative and Foundational to Our Faith 113
Appendix: Contemporary Accounts of the First Vision 129
Sources 141
Notes 149
Index 159

PREFACE

Beginnings are vital. No one can understand The Church of Jesus Christ of Latter-day Saints without looking seriously at the Church's beginnings. No one will get to the heart of the restored gospel, or to the hearts and minds of the people, who does not pay especial attention to how it all was started.

The founding event in The Church of Jesus Christ of Latter-day Saints is what has come to be known as Joseph Smith's First Vision. To be sure, a Christian's highest allegiance must always be to God, with faith centered in the divine Sonship of Jesus Christ. There is, however, a very real sense in which believing Latter-day Saints must have faith in the First Vision. That faith is based on testimony, on conviction, on an assurance that comes to individuals only by the power of God's Holy Spirit.

Our testimony and our devotion must be kept current. While Christ is and will forevermore be the center of our faith (our salvation depends upon it), true disciples of Christ are to be loyal to the men the Savior has called as apostles and prophets in their day. To accept the words and teachings of the prophets is to accept the words and teachings of the Savior himself (see Matthew 10:40; Doctrine and Covenants 1:38; 21:4–6; 112:20). It would follow, then, that to reject those who have been called to be prophets, seers, and revelators is to reject the Lord who sent them. In terms of the First Vision, such faith comes in the form of *trust* that what Joseph Smith claimed to have taken place in a grove of trees in upstate New York actually took place; *confidence* that young Joseph told the truth about what he beheld and what he learned; and *reliance* upon that information and that experience in understanding life's purpose and pursuing a strait path to everlasting life.

President Gordon B. Hinckley once observed that Joseph Smith's First Vision "is *the pivotal thing of our story*. Every claim that we make concerning divine authority, every truth that we offer concerning the validity of this work, all finds its root in the First Vision of the boy prophet. *Without it we would not have anything much to say*. This was the great curtain-raiser on the dispensation of the fullness of times, when God promised he would restore all the power, the gifts, the blessings, of all great dispensations in one great summing up."[1] On another occasion, President Hinckley bore testimony that "Joseph Smith saw the Father and the Son in the Sacred Grove. . . . It happened. It was real. If the First Vision occurred, then everything else in connection with the restoration occurred also. That is the great keystone of our faith and our testimony."[2]

President Ezra Taft Benson testified that "when God the Father and his Son Jesus Christ come to earth, as they did in 1820 when they appeared to the young boy prophet, Joseph Smith, it is not something that concerns only a handful of people. It is a message and a revelation intended for all of our Father's children living upon the face of the earth. It was the greatest event that ever happened in this world since the resurrection of the Master. Sometimes I think we are so close to it that we don't fully appreciate its significance and importance and the magnitude of it. The first vision of the Prophet Joseph Smith is bedrock theology in the Church."[3]

This book is about that vision of Joseph Smith. It focuses principally on the truths, doctrine, precepts, and guiding principles that derive from that vision. What did young Joseph learn, and what do we learn? Knowing, as President Boyd K. Packer taught many years ago, that "true doctrine, understood, changes attitudes and behavior,"[4] what doctrinal truths do we discover as we look deeply into different accounts of the First Vision? How does that doctrine affect the way we understand and approach our Heavenly Father and how we accept the atoning work of his Son, Jesus Christ? What does Brother Joseph's sacred and singular encounter in the Grove teach us about seeking for and obtaining divine guidance and personal revelation? How can such doctrine affect our view of life in this world, as well as the life we yearn to enjoy in the world to come? These are but examples of questions to which we will seek answers as we study and ponder carefully the accounts of the Prophet Joseph Smith's First Vision, along with prophetic commentary on the Prophet's monumental discovery.

As with any project of this kind, I am indebted to many people. In the fall of 1969, Professor Paul Cheesman of the Religious Education faculty at Brigham Young University first introduced me and other members of our Church History class to the various accounts of the First Vision. The testimony of a beloved friend, Robert J. Matthews, of the reality of Joseph Smith's First Vision as well as the larger Restoration stimulated my mind and stirred my soul over the years. On several occasions Bob and I spent precious time together in the Sacred Grove reading Joseph Smith's testimony of his vision, reflecting, conversing, and praying. I am also deeply grateful for all that I learned from colleagues—dedicated, inspired, and informed religious educators at BYU—during the thirty-one years I taught there. If I may borrow from the words of Oliver Cowdery, those were "days never to be forgotten" (Joseph Smith–History 1:71, footnote).

My friend and associate Von Memory has once again been extremely helpful in reading the manuscript and offering valuable recommendations on how to make this a better book. I express appreciation to Lisa Roper and the competent staff at Deseret Book Company, who shepherded this project from concept to completion. Special thanks is extended to Suzanne Brady and Derk Koldewyn for their excellent editorial work on the manuscript. And, as always, my dearest friend and eternal companion, Shauna, has been my inspiration and example of Christlike love and abiding commitment to the restored gospel and Church of Jesus Christ.

And now, although I am genuinely thankful for any and all assistance in researching and writing this book, I alone am responsible for the conclusions drawn from the evidence cited. While I have sought earnestly in my writing to be in harmony with holy scripture and the teachings of latter-day prophets, this volume is a private endeavor and not an official publication of The Church of Jesus Christ of Latter-day Saints.

Chapter 1

HOW IT ALL BEGAN

On 27 February 1967 my plane arrived in New York City, the headquarters of the Eastern States Mission, where I had been called to serve. Our group of eight missionaries spent a little over a day at the mission home, which was then located at 973 Fifth Avenue. During those hours we received an orientation to the life and work of full-time missionaries. In the evening, we enjoyed a lovely dinner, followed by a testimony meeting. The next morning we were introduced to our missionary companions and informed where we would be serving. I learned that I was assigned to work right in the City with three other missionaries for about four weeks, after which I would receive a more "permanent" assignment.

AN OVERWHELMING ASSIGNMENT

I had been in the City for only a matter of days when on a Tuesday morning I was told that we would be conducting a street meeting. I had no idea what a street meeting was. When I asked my companion for an explanation, he indicated that I would learn soon enough. At about 11:30 that morning we left our apartment and traveled to the corner of Wall Street and Nassau, to a spot right across the street from the New York Stock Exchange. The more seasoned elders began setting up the "Signs of the True Church" panel boards and placing a wooden box in a conspicuous place. At 11:55 a.m. our zone leader turned to me and said, "Elder, in five minutes a bell will ring and people who work across the street will pour out of the doors for lunch. Quite a number will make their way over to where we are. Most of them will listen to our message and then raise their questions." This was pretty exciting! It sounded like something Heber C. Kimball or Parley P. Pratt or B. H. Roberts did as they went out to spread the word of the restored gospel.

My excitement faded quickly as the zone leader then said to me, "Now, Elder Millet, step up on that box and teach us."

I asked what I was supposed to teach, and he replied, "The Apostasy and the Restoration."

I made my way to the box and stood as erect as I could. I then inquired, "Who am I speaking to, since all of you (a total of six missionaries) already know what I'm about to say?"

"Teach us anyway," our leader responded. "We will have a crowd for you to address in a couple of minutes."

As I reflect back on what took place more than half a century ago, I can still feel some of the emotional trauma and sense of absolute ineptness that filled my mind and heart that cold winter morning.

I looked about and took in the scene: New York City with its eight million people, ten thousand taxies blaring their horns, masses of men and women rushing about, venders selling their roasted chestnuts and their hot dogs, smog and pollution filling the air. A timid Louisiana kid who had never been away from home for more than a week (and then only for Scout camp) had been charged to speak, to teach, to somehow represent the Lord Jesus Christ and his Church to men of high station, many of whom had college degrees in finance, accounting, economics, and no doubt several held MBAs from Columbia, Harvard, Yale, or Stanford. When I now recall that frightening occasion, I am reminded of what the apostle Paul taught: "God hath chosen the foolish things of the world to confound the wise; and God hath chosen the weak things of the world to confound the things which are mighty" (1 Corinthians

1:27; compare Doctrine and Covenants 1:19). I certainly felt weak and simple. And I felt very alone.

On the stroke of noon, the bell rang and the building across the street emptied. And, as my leader had foretold, a large number of people began to cross the street and join us. It seemed like about a hundred people, but the number was probably closer to thirty. I was so nervous that I couldn't remember my name, but the Lord was gracious, and within thirty seconds all that I had studied about the Apostasy and the Restoration began to flood into my mind, bit by bit. And so I began to speak to the crowd. My knees were weak and my voice was shaky, but I stood and delivered what surely must have been a terribly profound discourse for some five or six minutes. I then stepped down from the box and noticed that the other missionaries were conversing with several of our visitors. Before I could make much sense of what was going on, a gentleman in a dark suit made his way over to me.

He asked a question something like, "I hear that you Mormons believe that you can become like God. Is that true?"

I was stunned by the question. I had supposed he might ask me about how the priesthood was lost or how the golden plates were translated, but he focused his question on one of the deepest and possibly most controversial matters in the faith and teachings of The Church of Jesus Christ of Latter-day Saints. Fortunately I didn't know a great deal about that subject, and so I remained silent. I was praying inwardly for something I might say, anything that might satisfy this man's curiosity. I remember looking him in the eye and saying, "That's a really good question. Let me see how I can begin to answer it." At this point I saw in my mind's eye a young boy kneeling in prayer in a lovely grove of trees. I took the idea and ran with it.

As I recall, I said, "Our story actually begins in upstate New York in the spring of 1820. It's an exciting story about a young boy by the name of Joseph Smith, who was confused about religion. He wanted to belong to a church, but he couldn't decide which one he should join.

And so he went into the woods to pray, to ask his Heavenly Father what he should do."

The man to whom I was speaking was kind and patient enough to allow me to tell the story of our beginnings—how it all started. Then he thanked me and walked away. It would be many years before I realized what I had done as a very green and frightened Latter-day Saint missionary and why I had done it. I have come to understand that sometimes we need to help our questioners ask the right questions.

As President Boyd K. Packer taught many years ago, in some situations we need to *answer the question the inquirer should have asked*.[1] This is not at all an effort to deceive or to be evasive but instead to acknowledge that there is a system of gospel prerequisites in teaching and learning about the gospel, a need to teach some things before others, in order to avoid confusion and misunderstanding. It is a principle that the Savior himself observed in his teachings (Matthew 13:10–11; JST, Matthew 7:9–11; JST, Matthew 21:34; Mark 4:10–11). It is a safe and proper avenue whereby you and I can move more quickly to the heart of our distinctive message—to that information that is foundational, that which is most important for those not of our faith to understand at that point in time.

An account of a conversation between Peter and Clement of Rome is particularly insightful in this regard. Peter counseled: "The teaching of all doctrine has a certain order: there are some things which must be delivered first, others in the second place, and others in the third, and so all in their order; and if these things be delivered in their order, they become plain; but *if they be brought forward out of order, they will seem to be spoken against reason*."[2] The man who posed the question to me seemed to be a decent sort of fellow, as well as a very bright person, but he really didn't need to know about deification, or *theosis*—how men and women become gods.

The truly significant issue facing this man, and the religious world today in general, is this: Was Joseph Smith called of God to be a latter-day prophet? Did the Father and the Son actually appear to him in the Sacred Grove in 1820? We must start there. We must always start there. In 1844 Brother Joseph put it this way: "If we start right, it is very easy for us to go right all the time. But if we start wrong, it is hard to get right."[3] I couldn't have known or understood as a brand-new missionary the significant principle taught by my late colleague Joseph Fielding McConkie: Members of the Church—all of whom are called to be missionaries—"will answer investigators' questions by *finding the simplest and most direct route to the Sacred Grove.*"[4]

THE DISPENSATION HEAD

God has always desired to communicate with his earthly children, especially as they prepare themselves properly for that encounter. Those chosen by him as his spokesmen or mouthpieces are called prophets. The prophets are called to be both *legal administrators* and *revealers of doctrinal truth*. "There is no salvation between the two lids of the Bible without a legal administrator," Joseph Smith taught.[5]

"A gospel dispensation is a period of time in which the Lord has at least one authorized servant on the earth who bears the keys of the holy priesthood."[6] We really do not know how many dispensations there have been since the beginning of time, but we usually speak of seven major dispensations: the dispensations of Adam, Enoch, Noah, Abraham, Moses, Jesus Christ, and Joseph Smith.

"You start out with the Lord Jesus," Elder Bruce R. McConkie declared, "and then you have Adam and Noah. Thereafter come the dispensation heads. Then you come to the prophets, to apostles, to the elders of Israel, and to wise and good and sagacious men who have the spirit of light and understanding. Every dispensation head is a revealer of Christ for his day; every prophet is a witness of Christ; and every other prophet or apostle who comes is a reflection and an echo and an exponent of the dispensation head. All such come to echo to the world and to expound and unfold what God has revealed through the man who was appointed for that era. Such is the dispensation concept."[7] In short, *the dispensation head is the preeminent prophetic revealer to the world of Jesus Christ and the plan of salvation.*

Joseph Smith was foreordained and called to see the face of God, receive divine instruction and priesthood authority, and set in motion a restoration that is destined to be a grand revolution.[8] As Brother Joseph stated, "It is in the order of heavenly things that God should always send a new dispensation into the world when men have apostatized from the truth and lost the priesthood."[9] Joseph was appointed to be the head of the dispensation of the fulness of times, the dispensation of the fulness of dispensations.

In an inspired letter written by Joseph to the Saints in Nauvoo, he pointed out that "it is necessary in the ushering in of the dispensation of the fulness of times, which dispensation is now beginning to usher in, that a whole and complete and perfect union, and welding together of dispensations, and keys, and powers, and glories should take place, and be revealed from the days of Adam even to the present time. And not only this, but *those things which never have been revealed from the foundation of the world, but have been kept hid from the wise and prudent, shall be revealed unto babes and sucklings in this, the dispensation of the fulness of times*" (Doctrine and Covenants 128:18; emphasis added; see also 121:26; 124:41).

VISIONS IN THE LIFE OF FAITH

Great truths, powerful doctrine, and supernal and enduring precepts are to be learned from a careful study of the First Vision of Joseph Smith the Prophet, what some have called "the Theophany in Palmyra." A *theophany* is a manifestation from God, a sacred occasion when God manifests himself to mortal men and women. And that's exactly what happened to a fourteen-year-old boy who needed answers to his all-important questions.

Visions have been a significant means by which our Father in Heaven has communicated with his children through the generations. When we think of visions, we automatically reflect on the heaven-sent experiences of prophets such as Enoch (Moses 6–7), Abraham (John 8:56; Helaman 8:17; JST, Genesis 15:9–12), Moses (Moses 1), King Nebuchadnezzar (Daniel 2), Lehi and Nephi (1 Nephi 8, 11–14), Stephen (Acts 7:55–56), Saul of Tarsus (Acts 9:1–8; 22:1–11; 26:12–19), John the Beloved (Revelation), Joseph Smith (Joseph Smith–History 1:15–20; Doctrine and Covenants 6, 13, 76, 107:93, 110, 137), and Joseph F. Smith (Doctrine and Covenants 138). For a time these men were permitted and empowered to see "things which [are] not visible to the natural eye" (Moses 6:36). Ammon explained to King Limhi that "a seer can know of things which are past, and also of things which are to come, and by them [seers] shall all things be revealed, or, rather, shall secret things be made manifest, and hidden things shall come to light, and things which are not known shall be made known by them which otherwise could not be known" (Mosiah 8:17).

Was what Joseph Smith experienced in the Sacred Grove a *vision* or a *visitation*? Alex Baugh, a valued associate and professor of Church History and Doctrine at Brigham Young University, explained to BYU students that "visions can take various forms, including *a personal visitation or the appearance* of deity or heavenly angels." A personal visitation was, in fact, what fourteen-year-old Joseph Smith experienced in the woods near his father's farm. "In another type of vision," Brother Baugh continued, "the veil is lifted from a person's mind and their spiritual eyes behold the things of God. This [latter] kind of vision might be called *a mind vision*." He went on to say that "in a mind vision no divine personages are present, even though they might be seen. A mind vision might also include being able to see scenes of heaven or past, present, and future events. The revelation that is now Doctrine and Covenants 76 [the vision of the degrees of glory] is an example of this type of manifestation."[10]

In discussing the First Vision, Elder John A. Widtsoe pointed out that "there was of course nothing impossible or improbable in the event. In the Christian faith lies embedded the doctrine that God is the framer of the heavens and the earth, the creator of man on earth. Such a personage cannot be divested of the right to come on earth, to show himself to his children, or to set his work in order. He has done so before; he may do so at his pleasure, or at any time. It is a type of blasphemy to say that he cannot do so."[11]

ACCOUNTS OF THE FIRST VISION

The four primary accounts of Joseph Smith's First Vision were written or dictated by the Prophet Joseph Smith. The earliest account, written in the second half of 1832, is part of Joseph's early autobiography, contained within the earliest history of the Church and written largely by the Prophet himself.[12]

The second recounting of his vision took place about three years later on 9 November 1835. We read the following in the "Manuscript History of the Church": "While sitting in my house between ten and eleven this morning a man came in and introduced himself to me, calling himself by the name of 'Joshua, the Jewish minister.' . . . We soon commenced talking on the subject of religion; and after I had made some remarks concerning the Bible, I commenced giving him a relation of the circumstances connected with the coming forth of the Book of Mormon."[13] The man's real name was Robert Matthias or Robert Matthews, and it was during this conversation that the Prophet related his 1820 experience in the Sacred Grove. The account was dictated to Warren Parrish.

The third, or 1838–1839, account (which we will refer to as the 1838 account) is the official account of the vision that is part of Joseph Smith–History in the Pearl of Great Price. It is the most complete account and contains many details not found in the others. The account first appeared in the *Times and Seasons* on 15 March 1842. The scribe was James Mulholland.[14]

A man by the name of George Barstow, who was writing a history of New Hampshire, contacted his friend John Wentworth, editor of the *Chicago Democrat*, and requested information about the rise of The Church of Jesus Christ of Latter-day Saints. Wentworth communicated with Joseph and asked for the information. The result was a letter from the Prophet that has come to be known as the Wentworth letter (1842). It contains a brief history of the Church, including an account of the First Vision. This history was first published in the Nauvoo newspaper the *Times and Seasons* on 1 March 1842.

We are also blessed to have in our possession several secondary accounts—Joseph's descriptions of his vision recorded by others. We will draw upon Orson Pratt's 1840 account, which was contained in a pamphlet entitled *An Interesting Account of Several Remarkable Visions, and of the Late Discovery of Ancient American Records*. This account has the distinction of being the first published account, prepared by Elder Pratt while he was on a mission in Scotland.

In addition, we have an account written by Elder Orson Hyde in 1842. On his way to dedicate the land of Palestine as a gathering place for the descendants of Abraham, Isaac, and Jacob, Elder Hyde prepared a booklet, written in German but whose title in English is *A Cry from the Wilderness, a Voice from the Dust of the Earth*. He seems to have borrowed a good bit of detail from Orson Pratt's account.

Two other secondary accounts that we will draw upon include one by David Nye White, editor of the *Pittsburgh Weekly Gazette*, who interviewed Joseph Smith (1843); and one by Alexander Neibaur, a Jewish convert to the Church from England. Neibaur heard Joseph Smith relate his experience not long before the martyrdom (1844).[15] I have chosen not to include the account of Levi Richards (1843), simply because it is so brief and does not contribute any new understanding about what Joseph learned and experienced. The Richards account is available at ChurchofJesusChrist.org/Gospel Topics/First Vision Accounts.

We will draw upon these eight contemporary accounts in reconstructing the singular and significant event of Joseph Smith's First Vision as we seek to discover truths about God, Jesus Christ, Joseph Smith, and the manner in which the Almighty chose to initiate this final dispensation. For ease in reading, I have modernized the punctuation and spelling in these eight documents, which are found in the appendix at the end of this volume. The accounts in their original form are available at ChurchofJesusChrist.org.

That sacred appearance, that vision-visitation in Palmyra, is the foundation on which the Restoration is built. It is the beginning of the revelation of God to humankind in these last days. Ours is a time foreseen by holy men and women for generations and centuries, a pivotal moment when righteousness would be sent down from heaven and truth would spring forth out of the earth (see, for example, Psalm 85:11; 2 Nephi 3:6–15; Mormon 8:16, 25; Moses 7:62).

Joseph Smith's First Vision represents the opening of the divine door to principles and doctrine and practices that are almost without number. Through the call of Joseph Smith, the "choice seer" (2 Nephi 3:6), "God has provided a means that man, through faith, might work mighty miracles; therefore he [the seer] becometh a great benefit to his fellow beings" (Mosiah 8:18).

Chapter 2

THE WINDS OF REVIVALISM

*I*n a world like our own, where millions upon millions of persons throughout the earth have voted against religion and religious denominations with their feet—by walking away[1]—it may be difficult for some of us to imagine a time in America's history when masses of people seemed to be impelled to "get religion," to find a church to join.

SPIRITUAL AWAKENINGS

The United States had passed through the Age of Enlightenment in the eighteenth century, when individuals were encouraged to put away age-old superstitions, exalt human reason, and find truth through empirical study and the application of the scientific method. A spirit of bold independence characterized the mood of the time, as liberated citizens sought to cast off the shackles of tradition, to cut themselves free from traditional religious, political, and other restraints. The breaking free of political restraints is illustrated in the events of the American Revolutionary War. The breaking free of religious restraints prepared many to be receptive to the message of the Restoration.

During that same period of time, sections of England and New England were passing through what came to be known as the "First Great Awakening." That era featured such notable persons as Jonathan

Edwards, a Reformed (Calvinist) preacher-theologian in New England who is perhaps best known for his fiery sermon "Sinners in the Hands of an Angry God"; George Whitefield, also Reformed but characterized by a gentle and contagious charisma that drew persons from many, many miles away to set aside everything else to hear him; and John Wesley, the father of Methodism and one of the most gifted and persistent circuit riders of the eighteenth century. He spoke of total sanctification and urged his followers to strive for Christian perfection. Such religious figures as these preached to thousands upon thousands of men and women eager to forsake their sins and be put into proper relationship with Deity.

By the nineteenth century, the pendulum had begun to swing in a different direction. As a kind of reaction to what many considered to be the cold and calculating perspective of a world governed wholly by reason, the spirit of Romanticism encouraged people to look to their feelings, attend to their innermost desires, trust in the Transcendent. "Such sentiments were no longer suspect or frowned upon as they had been in the past," historian Robert Remini observed. "Now they were believed to aid individuals in their search for truth and wisdom. Intuition also served as a tool in their search. . . .

"As this romantic impulse swept across the United States," Remini continued, "it helped shape American attitudes about religion," namely that "every person could achieve salvation through his or her own volition by submitting to the lordship of Christ. All it took to win salvation was an act of the will and the desire to obey the commandments and lead a holy life. The idea of an elect chosen by God [the Calvinistic or Reformed doctrine of predestination] no longer had the same force it enjoyed in the colonial era."[2]

The first three decades of the nineteenth century became known as the "Second Great Awakening." One of the most colorful personalities of the time, especially between 1825 and 1835 in upstate New York and also in Manhattan was Charles Grandison Finney, known as the father of modern revivalism. Because many of Finney's methods and influence continued into the twentieth century, it might be worthwhile to speak of him in a bit more detail. "Born in Connecticut," one historian wrote, "he was raised in upstate New York, and became first a school teacher and then a lawyer. After his conversion, he abruptly forsook his law practice to take up 'a retainer from the Lord Jesus Christ to plead his cause.' Although lacking in formal theological education and a bit vague on certain doctrinal matters, Finney managed to inveigle a local presbytery to ordain him and began a new life as a preacher.

"Although sponsored by the Presbyterians, Finney's course was much too independent to be restricted by any denomination. He preached wherever he could, focusing on the Burned-Over District he already knew well.[3] Finney soon attracted attention through his employment of 'New Measures Revivalism,' which was largely of his own devising. One of these new measures that raised many eyebrows was the 'anxious bench,' a seat placed near the revivalist on which those who appeared to be on the brink of conversion could be placed and worked on intensively. Pressure for conversion was intensified by another measure, the 'protracted meeting,' which stretched on for hours at a time and often was continued on succeeding days. Women openly testifying at meetings and Finney's praying by name for his antagonists were still other innovations that were less than universally welcomed."[4]

One of my history professors at Florida State University commented that "Charles Grandison Finney was to revivalism what Fanny Farmer was to cookbooks." That is, Finney devised a methodology, a technique, a formula, a template of sorts on how to carry out a successful revival. One of his books, *Revival Lectures*, is a handbook to bringing souls to Christ. Finney stressed the importance of human action and thus the need for individuals to "make a decision for Christ," an expression and an idea that was later employed most successfully in the twentieth-century revivals of the world famous and beloved evangelist Billy Graham.

Peter Cartwright, an American Methodist revivalist, wrote, "The great mass of our Western people wanted a preacher that could mount a stump, a block, or old log, or stand in the bed of a wagon, and, without note or manuscript, quote, expound, and apply the word of God to the hearts and consciences of the people."[5]

CHRISTIAN PRIMITIVISM

The Second Great Awakening was also the age of Restorationism, often called Christian Primitivism, a time in America's history when men and women sought for a return to the ancient order of things. Many longed for the reestablishment of primitive Christianity; others desired to enjoy once more the spiritual gifts and outpourings that had once graced the ancients in New Testament times. A prominent example of one imbued with Restorationist desires was the Irish-born Alexander Campbell. He accepted the doctrine of believer's baptism by immersion (for accountable persons only), was baptized, and in 1811 accepted the pastorate at the Brush Run Baptist Church in what is now Bethany, West Virginia.

Campbell's adherence to his Restorationist beliefs proved a serious concern to Baptists, and he was rejected by many Baptist colleagues in the ministry. Campbell's dissatisfaction with nominal Christianity is apparent in a statement from the first volume of a magazine he began called the *Christian Baptist*: "We are convinced, fully convinced, that the whole head is sick, and the whole heart faint of modern fashionable Christianity."[6] In addition, Campbell, an iconoclast, "condemned all beliefs and practices that could not be validated by apostolic mandates. He proclaimed that missionary societies, tract societies, Bible societies, synods, associations, and theological seminaries were inconsistent with pure religion."[7]

In 1838 Ralph Waldo Emerson stated in his famous "Divinity School Address" at Harvard that "the need was never greater of new revelation than now." Further, "the Church seems to totter to its fall, almost all life extinct." Continuing, Emerson said, "I look for the hour when that supreme Beauty, which ravished the souls of those eastern men, and chiefly of those Hebrews, and through their lips spoke oracles to all time, shall speak in the West also."[8]

Sidney Rigdon became a close associate of Alexander Campbell before discovering the restored gospel. Sidney would become a servant in the hands of the Lord, a kind of Elias or forerunner: "Behold thou wast sent forth, even as John [the Baptist], to prepare the way before me, and before Elijah which should come, and thou knewest it not" (Doctrine and Covenants 35:4). Sidney received the message of the Restoration himself, and he and his wife, Phebe, were baptized on 14 November 1830. He then rushed back enthusiastically to his congregations in Ohio to deliver the glad tidings. Individuals such as Sidney Rigdon and Parley P. Pratt, who had come to know Rigdon quite well before he discovered the gospel fulness, went on to become powerful and influential spokesmen for the new revelation.

A VISIONARY CULTURE

Some of the best-known, memorized, and quoted verses of Restoration scripture are found in Doctrine and Covenants 4, a revelation given to Joseph Smith Sr. in February 1829. It begins with "Now behold, a marvelous work is about to come forth among the children of men." Later in this short revelation, the Lord states that "the field is white already to harvest" (verses 1, 4). The God who knows all things from beginning to end had been laying a foundation for that religious revolution we call the Restoration. This "marvelous work and a wonder" was not to take place without immense and intricate preparation on the part of the Almighty. People would be in place. Concepts and points of view would be in the air. Hearts would be open to a new revelation in an unprecedented manner. Nothing was to be left to chance.

Jehovah had spoken through the prophet Joel in ancient times: "It shall come to pass afterward, that I will pour out my spirit upon all flesh; and your sons and your daughters shall prophesy, your old men shall dream dreams, your young men shall see visions: and also upon the servants and upon the handmaids in those days will I pour out my spirit" (Joel 2:28–29). In an important article published in *Brigham Young University Studies* in 1997 entitled "The Visionary World of Joseph Smith," Latter-day Saint historian Richard L. Bushman wrote of instance after instance in which men and women in the late eighteenth and early nineteenth centuries enjoyed dreams, visions, and other divine manifestations. We know of the role such dreams had in the preparation of the Joseph Smith Sr. family, preparation for what would come to pass through the instrumentality of Joseph Smith Jr.[9] Bushman described some thirty-two pamphlets "that relate visionary experiences published in the United States between 1783 and 1815." He added that "experiences in England and Canada were on a par with those from the United States. . . . Gender and social class figured scarcely at all in the accounts. . . . The pamphlets were virtually oblivious to social class."[10]

> This "marvelous work and a wonder" was not to take place without immense and intricate preparation on the part of the Almighty. People would be in place. Concepts and points of view would be in the air. Hearts would be open to a new revelation in an unprecedented manner. Nothing was to be left to chance.

Professor Bushman distinguished Joseph Smith's experience and its effects upon people from those of the many claiming to have spoken to loved ones who had died, to have seen angels that appeared, and even to have received visions of Jesus. He asked the question whether some of these reported visions were premonitions of "what was to come or in some way a preparation for a later revelation of God?" In answer to his own question, Bushman referred to a Methodist named Solomon Chamberlain who had remarkable experiences of the sort we have mentioned here (and who later joined The Church of Jesus Christ of Latter-day Saints and died in Utah). He proposed that "Chamberlain's visions readied him to believe visions and to accept the Book of Mormon without the doubts that impeded most Americans. Did the visionary culture open the minds of others? Can we imagine little gleams of light breaking through the clouds everywhere, as a preliminary to the fulness of the Restoration?"[11]

In speaking of a man named Norris Stearns, Bushman said that "Stearns proclaimed himself a prophet, but he did not go on to organize a church. His writings did not become scripture or attract believers. Nor did the writings of any of the other thirty-one pamphleteers. People did not flock to hear the visionaries' teachings or pull up roots to gather with believers. Followers of Joseph Smith did all these things and more. They reoriented their entire lives to comply with his revelations. *The differences are so great,*" Bushman concluded, "*that we can scarcely even say Joseph was the most successful of the visionaries; taking his life as a whole, he was of another species.*"[12]

A TUMULT OF OPINIONS

If you will, sketch a mental picture of the religious landscape of upstate New York between 1800 and 1830. What was it like? For one thing, less than 15 percent of the population of the United States were affiliated with any church. In an effort to become grounded once again in a particular faith tradition, many people began to search for a church to join. The priests and ministers of the time must have rejoiced over this religious yearning, this universal longing, this quest for truth and salvation, as a prime time for widespread conversion.

DeWitt Clinton, governor of New York, provided the following account of these tumultuous times: "We stopped in a road to see a camp-meeting of Methodists. . . .

"Here, eating and drinking was going on; there, people were drying themselves by a fire. . . . At length four preachers ascended the pulpit, and the orchestra was filled with forty more. The people, about two hundred in number, were called together by a trumpet. . . . A good-looking man opened the service with prayer. . . . After prayer he commenced a sermon, the object of which was to prove the utility of preaching up the terrors of hell, as necessary to arrest the attention of the audience to the arguments of the ministers. . . . As far as we could hear, the voice of the preacher, growing louder and louder, reached our ears as we departed, and we met crowds of people going to the sermon. On the margin of the road, we saw persons with cakes, beer, and other refreshments for sale."[13]

The Joseph Smith Sr. family was divided religiously. Mother Smith was drawn toward Presbyterianism and the tenets of Calvinism. As we know from Joseph Jr.'s own words, Lucy Mack Smith and three of the children (Hyrum, Samuel Harrison, and Sophronia) joined that church (Joseph Smith–History 1:7). Father Smith felt suspicious of most organized religion. Joseph Sr. and his father, Asael Smith, "came to believe that God was much more loving than they had been taught in church. They rejected the Calvinist idea of limited atonement. 'Jesus Christ,' Asael told his family, 'can as well save all, as any.' This way of thinking became known as Universalism, and Asael and his son Joseph Sr. organized a Universalist Society the year after Joseph and Lucy were married."[14]

"Neither of [Joseph's] parents were securely tied to any of the main Christian groups of the region," respected historian Grant Wacker wrote. "The senior Smith considered himself something of a free thinker, but he was never too sure about his unbelief. Joseph's mother, Lucy Mack Smith, regarded herself a Presbyterian, but she also seemed unclear of her commitments. For Lucy, too many different groups claimed to know the truth. Joseph [Jr.] inherited his parents' uncertainty about the current religious choices. But more than either of them he determined to settle the truth for himself."[15]

Young Joseph was attracted to the Methodists, by his own report (Joseph Smith–History 1:8). Methodists, followers of John Wesley, were Arminian in their beliefs, that is, they believed in the freedom of the will and that individuals had a significant role to play in their own salvation. Joseph Jr. attended many of the camp meetings with his family. According to Alexander Neibaur's 1844 account of the First Vision, Joseph's "mother and brother and sister got religion. He wanted to get religion too; he wanted to feel and shout like the rest, but could feel nothing."[16]

It might be worthwhile to reflect on how young Joseph Smith described the "war of words and tumult of opinions" that he and his family experienced. In his 1835 account of the vision, Joseph remarked that "being wrought up in my mind respecting the subject of religion and looking at the different systems taught the children of men, I knew not who was right or who was wrong, and I considered it of first importance that I should be right, in matters that involve eternal consequences; being thus perplexed in mind, I retired to the silent grove."[17]

> Joseph's "mother and brother and sister got religion. He wanted to get religion too; he wanted to feel and shout like the rest, but could feel nothing."
> —Alexander Neibaur

In the official account of the First Vision (1838), found in the Pearl of Great Price, the Prophet Joseph pointed out that "there was in the place where we lived an unusual excitement on the subject of religion. It commenced with the Methodists, but soon became general among all the sects. . . . Great multitudes united themselves to the different religious parties, which created no small stir and division amongst the people, some crying, 'Lo, here!' and others, 'Lo, there!' Some were contending for the Methodist faith, some for the Presbyterian, and some for the Baptist." He added that "when the converts began to file off, some to one party and some to another, it was seen that the seemingly good feelings of both the priests and the converts were more pretended than real; for a scene of great confusion and bad feeling ensued" (Joseph Smith–History 1:5–6).

Finally, in the Wentworth letter (1842), Joseph explained that "when about fourteen years of age I began to reflect upon the importance of being prepared for a future state." In his quest, he "found that there was a great clash in religious sentiment." Sensing "that all could not be right, and that God could not be the author of so much confusion, I determined to investigate the subject more fully, believing that if God had a church it would not be split up into factions, and that if he taught one society to worship one way, and administer in one set of ordinances, he would not teach another principles which were diametrically opposed."[18]

WHAT WERE THE CONTESTED DOCTRINES?

What were they arguing about? What are some topics that might have kept the fiery rhetoric and unchristian behavior alive and bubbling? Consider for a moment some of the doctrinal subjects about which the various religious denominations might then have differed and disagreed, topics about which many still disagree today:

- Whether God is completely sovereign (and thus responsible for) and in control of all that happens on earth, or whether persons have true freedom of the will and play a significant role in gaining salvation.
- Whether only the predestined are saved, or whether all have the potential for salvation.
- Whether individuals can enjoy eternal security once they are "saved," or whether they can fall from grace.
- What happens to the souls of babies who die.
- Whether Jesus Christ was both fully God and fully human during his mortal ministry, or whether he relinquished his divinity for a season.

- Whether Jesus Christ retains his resurrected physical body, or whether he is now a spirit in heaven.
- Whether men and women are totally depraved as a result of the Fall, or whether persons become carnal, sensual, and devilish as a result of sinful deeds.
- Whether a person is saved solely by grace, solely by works, or by both grace and works.
- Whether ordinances or sacraments, especially baptism, are essential for salvation.
- Whether baptism should be by sprinkling, pouring, or immersion.
- Whether children should be baptized, or whether only accountable persons should be baptized.
- Whether the bread and the water (or wine) for the Sacrament of the Lord's Supper literally becomes the body and blood of Jesus Christ, or whether the bread and the water (or wine) of the sacrament are used simply in remembrance of him.
- Whether the Atonement of Jesus Christ is efficacious only for those who are elect, or whether all may benefit from his atoning suffering.
- Whether one can accept Jesus as Savior but postpone until later a profession of him as Lord and Master.
- Whether one receives divine authority by simply accepting Christ as Savior, or whether that authority is conferred by the laying on of hands.
- Whether women should serve in certain ministerial capacities.
- Whether spiritual gifts (including both institutional and individual revelation) ceased with the deaths of the original apostles, or whether spiritual gifts are a crucial part of the body of Christ in all ages.
- Whether the Bible is inerrant—meaning, without error or flaw—or whether scribal errors took place during its long years of transmission.

- Whether the gathering of Israel is accomplished symbolically by individuals coming unto Christ, or whether the gathering of Abraham's descendants is a literal phenomenon.
- What happens at the time of death.
- The nature of tribulation, the Rapture, and the Millennium.

Incomplete though it is, that is a rather stunning list, is it not? In addition, the boy prophet found—and this must have been particularly disappointing, even painful to him—that "the teachers of religion of the different sects understood the same passages of scripture so differently as to destroy all confidence in settling the question by an appeal to the Bible" (Joseph Smith–History 1:12). How frustrating to discover that the Holy Bible, one element of Christianity that ought to unite men and women of faith everywhere, complicated rather than simplified the matter of which path was the proper one to pursue.[19]

> "For all their learning and their eloquence, the clergy could not be trusted with the Bible. They did not understand what the book meant. It was a record of revelations, and the ministry had turned it into a handbook."
> —Richard Bushman

Richard L. Bushman offered the following assessment of what Joseph faced and what he did: "At some level, Joseph's revelations indicate a loss of trust in the Christian ministry. For all their learning and their eloquence, the clergy could not be trusted with the Bible. They did not understand what the book meant. It was a record of revelations, and the ministry had turned it into a handbook. *The Bible had become a text to be interpreted rather than an experience to be lived.* In the process, the power of the book was lost."[20] And yet, amid the shouts and contortions of intense attenders of the camp meetings, large numbers of people made their way into one church or another. Research by Professor Milton V. Backman Jr. indicated that on 19 June 1818, a

Methodist camp meeting "was held near Palmyra which, according to one report, resulted in twenty baptisms and forty conversions to the Methodist society." Further, in the years 1819–20, the nearby towns of Geneva and Oaks Corners saw conversions numbering eighty and thirty, respectively.[21]

THE POWER OF A SCRIPTURAL PASSAGE

William Smith, youngest brother of the Prophet, stated in an interview that one evening, a Reverend George Lane preached a sermon on the question "which church should I join?" and focused on James 1:5.[22] "Like a flash of sunlight through lowering clouds," President George Q. Cannon wrote, "the import of a mighty truth burst upon Joseph's mind. He had vainly been asking help from men who had answered him out of their own darkness. He determined now to seek assistance from God. . . . He could not doubt [the promise], without doubting his Maker."[23]

And of course there is no more moving and descriptive statement regarding the power of pondering than that contained in the Prophet's own words: "Never did any passage of scripture come with more power to the heart of man than this did at this time to mine" (Joseph Smith–History 1:11–12). The message of James 1:5 "was cheering information to [Joseph]," Elder Orson Pratt concluded in his 1840 account of the First Vision, "tidings that gave him great joy. It was like a light shining forth in a dark place to guide him to the path in which he should walk."[24]

"A single sentence," Elder Bruce R. McConkie pointed out, "twenty-six plain and simple words—these Spirit-authored words have had a great impact upon religion and all that appertains to it. Though they present a divine concept of universal application, . . . yet they were preserved through the ages for the especial guidance of that prophet who should usher in the dispensation of the fulness of times."[25]

Notice that Joseph reflected on the scriptural words again and again, and he had confidence in the word of God. His was no superficial inquiry. Young Joseph took an idea, an expression written sometime around A.D. 50, and "likened it" to himself; he took James's words from their original New Testament context, sensing that they had specific reference, relevance, and application to him, a farm boy in upstate New York.

• • •

In the spring of 1820, religion was in the air in upstate New York. Good people, upright people, God-fearing people, sought in their own way to come to know their Heavenly Father and to understand his will for them. Young Joseph Smith, a genuine seeker after truth, found himself in the midst of religious fervor that, from his own perspective, bred and spread more confusion and distraction than inspiration and certainly generated more heat than light.

In later years, other Latter-day Saint leaders spoke of their own quest for truth and of the frustrations they felt before their encounter with the restored gospel. Brigham Young said: "My mind was open to conviction, and I knew that the Christian world had not the religion that Jesus and his Apostles taught. I knew that there was not a Bible Christian on earth within my knowledge."[26] On another occasion, President Young described the depth of his longing to find the fulness of the gospel: "The secret feeling of my heart was that I would be willing to crawl around the earth on my hands and knees, to see such a man as was Peter, Jeremiah, Moses, or any man that could tell me anything about God and heaven."[27] "I did not join any church," Wilford Woodruff explained, "believing that the Church of Christ in its true organization did not exist upon the earth."[28]

An early apostle of this dispensation, Orson Hyde, attested in his 1842 account of the First Vision that "nature had endowed [Joseph Smith] with a keen critical intellect, and so he looked through the lens of reason and common sense and with pity and contempt upon these systems of religion. . . . Consequently, he began in an attitude of faith his own investigation of the word of God, [feeling that it was] the best way to arrive at a knowledge of the truth."[29]

Truly, the God and Father of us all—a Being of perfect mercy and infinite love, who deigns always to dispense divine truth when people are prepared to receive it—would not allow such righteous yearnings to go unanswered. The heavens would be opened. In 1842 Brother Joseph remarked that "*the God of heaven has begun to restore the ancient order of His kingdom* unto His servants and His people,—a day in which all things are concurring to bring about the completion of the fullness of the Gospel, *a fullness of the dispensation of dispensations*, even the fullness of times."[30]

Chapter 3

ENTERING THE GROVE

Let's remind ourselves about how often the doctrine of The Church of Jesus Christ of Latter-day Saints is inextricably linked to historical moments, historical events, and thus historical sites. We realize that there is something deeply significant to what is often called "sacred space." Certain locations take on special meaning because something important happened there.

SACRED SPACE

The prophet-editor Mormon wrote: "And it came to pass that as many as did believe [Alma the Elder] did go forth to a place which was called Mormon. . . . Now, there was in Mormon a fountain of pure water, and Alma resorted thither, there being near the water a thicket of small trees, where he did hide himself in the daytime from the searches of the king" (Mosiah 18:4–5). Alma began to baptize these people in the Waters of Mormon, and this group became a "church in the wilderness," "the church of Christ," one of the first of its kind in the Nephite record (Mosiah 18:17). Alma organized the church, ordained priests to teach the people, generated a spirit of love and cooperation among the new members of the church, and taught them to "impart of their substance, every one according to that which he had. . . of their own free will" (Mosiah 18:27). Alma's converts "did walk uprightly before God, imparting to one another both temporally and spiritually according to their needs and their wants" (Mosiah 18:29).

Notice the tender words that follow: "And now it came to pass that all this was done in Mormon, yea, by the waters of Mormon, . . . *how beautiful are they to the eyes of them who there came to the knowledge of their Redeemer*; yea, and how blessed are they, for *they shall sing to his praise forever*" (Mosiah 18:30; emphasis added). These marvelous people would never forget what had taken place that day on that site. They would remember what they felt and what they experienced. Indeed, they would never forget the Waters of Mormon, the singular spot of ground that became hallowed to those who there received an unmistakable witness of the Spirit and became members of the Church of Jesus Christ by covenant and ordinance.

On one occasion I took my youngest son with me to Louisiana to visit family and friends. I had grown up in the Southern states, and it was there that I first went to church, was baptized, received the Aaronic and Melchizedek Priesthoods, and left on a mission. After we had visited with relatives and associates during the first few days of our trip, we headed north to the community where I attended high school. We came to a Latter-day Saint chapel and pulled into the large parking lot in front of the building.

We left the car, and he and I walked closer to the church building. My son asked, "Why are we here?"

I answered by telling him my story. I spoke of how when our small branch began to gather in this community, this particular spot of ground was essentially a swamp. I told him of the chicken dinners, the spaghetti dinners, the doughnut sales, the bazaars, even the rodeo we sponsored—all to raise funds to build the first phase of a church building, essentially a classroom facility. We walked over to the white block building that was Phase One, and I pointed out that I was one of many who had painted those walls, inside and out.

I described how we then began a whole series of new fund-raisers to build Phase Two, a beautiful chapel. I told him of how tough it was for a small group of us to lift those huge beams that supported the roof. I said that one day while walking tenuously on that very steep roof, I began to slide down and in the process snagged my leg on a nail. This meetinghouse was where I bore my testimony for the first time, I explained. This was the church where my dad had served as the first bishop of the ward and the place where I was taught the gospel by devoted members, faithful Saints who were highly schooled in the things of the Spirit. It was in that chapel that I delivered my farewell address before leaving on a mission.

Such sweet memories. I said to my son, "There is a part of me in that church building. And there is a big part of that building that is in me." It occurred to me that a significant part of my testimony of the restored gospel resides in my soul because I invested myself in that building and, more particularly, in *what took place in that building*. How beautiful that spot of earth has become to me. There's a good reason why I always drive to this spot each time I travel to the South to visit family. Through the medium of memory, I relive precious elements of testimony that were planted in my soul there in those formative years. That is to me hallowed ground, sacred space.

If you have visited the Holy Land, you understand perfectly what I mean when I speak of sacred space. I have heard scores of people say that after having walked where Jesus walked, they could never read the New Testament the same way again. They could never read Peter's declaration of testimony at Caesarea Philippi without envisioning the huge outcropping of rock in that location where Jesus stated that "upon this rock [meaning the rock of revelation[1]] I will build my church" (Matthew 16:18). They could never read the Savior's fervent plea to God, "O my Father, if it be possible, let this cup pass from me" (Matthew 26:39), without reflecting on the ancient olive trees they had stood among in the Garden of Gethsemane on the slopes of the Mount of Olives. And they certainly could never again read the Resurrection narratives without deep emotion in remembrance of that sacred and solemn time they had spent in the Garden Tomb. Sacred space carries with it a sacred feeling.

Some time ago my wife, Shauna, and I returned from an eleven-day Church history trip that I had been invited to lead. As our group of thirty-four stood in the Sacred Grove, I read from the various accounts of the First Vision, discussed the contributions of each, and considered what vital doctrinal answers had come as a result of Joseph Smith's crucial question. We spent time reflecting on what the Palmyra theophany would have meant to the fourteen-year-old boy, how he might have explained it to his parents and brothers and sisters, how pained he must have felt when ministers and prominent people rejected his claim on the basis that signs and gifts and wonders had ceased by the end of the first century. The Spirit that rested upon us while we were in the grove was one of pure peace, enlightenment, and conviction. We were standing near where one of the most significant events in all of recorded history took place. We knew and we felt that we were standing on holy ground.

We had similar experiences as we visited Fayette, New York, where the restored Church was organized; Harmony, Pennsylvania, where Joseph and Oliver received the Aaronic and Melchizedek Priesthoods and the holy apostleship; Hiram, Ohio, where the vision of the degrees of glory was received; the Kirtland Temple, where groups of Saints saw visions, spoke in tongues, and entertained angels. I could go on and on to speak of sacred, historic moments in such places as Adam-ondi-Ahman and Jackson County, Missouri, and Nauvoo, Illinois. In each of those sites, and many others, we were endued with a superintending Presence that bore witness of what had taken place there. In short, we were passing through sacred space.

THE EXACT LOCATION

Not even the brightest and best-schooled Latter-day Saint guides can in truth declare, "We know for certain that this is the actual site where Mary gave birth to Jesus" or "This is the exact spot where Jesus was baptized" or "It was right here that the resurrected Lord sat on the banks of the Sea of Galilee and taught his apostles." And yet we can still have a marvelous spiritual experience at a particular location when we contemplate on the miraculous virgin birth of the Savior of the world. We can sit on what is called today the Mount of Beatitudes, read from the Sermon on the Mount, and be deeply inspired by our Master's teachings, not knowing the exact place where those timeless truths were spoken but knowing that *they had indeed been spoken* somewhere near there. And we can stand at the site called by many the "place of the skull," or Golgotha, and reflect reverently and intensely on the agony and ignominy of the only perfect man ever to live on this planet, as he hung on the accursed cross—even if that is not the very ground that was soiled and stained by his precious, redeeming blood.

And so it is regarding what we call the Sacred Grove. No one (except the Lord and Joseph Smith) knows the exact spot where Joseph knelt or what section of the forest was brightened by the glory of the Father and the Son. And yet, anyone who has spent some time in the Sacred Grove, who has a conviction of the truthfulness of the restored gospel, can know, by the power of the Holy Spirit, that that world-changing and paradigm-shifting event did take place and that it was somewhere nearby.

Historian Donald L. Enders wrote that the grove is "part of the forest that once covered the Smiths' 100-acre farm in Manchester Township as well as much of western New York." More specifically, he said, "the forest was some 400 years old when the family of Joseph Smith, Sr., moved to the site in 1818 or 1819. The large trees of the forest—maple, beech, elm, oak, and hickory—reached heights of up to 125 feet and diameters of 6 feet or more. Beneath this natural canopy grew hop hornbeam, wild cherry, and ash. The woodland floor was carpeted with leaves, ferns, grasses, wildflowers, and clumps of chokecherry and dogwood." Finally, "the Smiths cleared the trees from sixty acres of their property. The Sacred Grove was part of a fifteen-acre wooded tract at the farm's west end, reserved as a sugarbush, where trees were tapped for making maple syrup and sugar."[2]

Somewhere in that vicinity, as David Nye White's 1843 account of the First Vision states, Joseph went "into the woods where my father had a clearing, and *went to the stump where I had stuck my axe when I had quit work*, and I kneeled down, and prayed."[3] The specificity of those words is a quiet but real affirmation that the boy prophet did in very deed have the divine encounter that took place moments later.

WHY JOSEPH ENTERED THE GROVE

The Prophet Joseph has provided for us one of the most compelling illustrations of the power of pondering and reflecting on holy scripture: "I was one day reading the epistle of James, first chapter and fifth verse, which reads: If any of you lack wisdom, let him ask of God, that giveth to all men liberally, and upbraideth not; and it shall be given him. Never did any passage of scripture come with more power to the heart of man than this did at this time to mine. It seemed to enter with great force into every feeling of my heart. I reflected on it again and again, knowing that if any person needed wisdom from God, I did; for how to act I did not know, and unless I could get more wisdom than I then had, I would never know" (Joseph Smith–History 1:11–12).

"The Holy Ghost is central to the Restoration," Elder Robert D. Hales reminded us. The power or spiritual impact the scriptural passage had on Joseph Smith "was the influence of the Holy Ghost. As a result, Joseph went into a grove of trees near his home and knelt down to ask of God. The First Vision that followed was truly momentous and magnificent. But the path to that in-person visitation of the Father and the Son began with a prompting from the Holy Ghost to pray.

"The revealed truths of the restored gospel came through the pattern of seeking in prayer and then receiving and following the promptings of the Holy Ghost."[4]

President Henry B. Eyring spoke similarly of this matter. "Joseph started for the grove to pray with faith that a loving God would answer his prayer and relieve his confusion. *He gained that assurance reading the word of God* [James 1:5] *and receiving a witness that it was true.* . . . His faith to ask of God in prayer came after pondering a scripture which assured him of God's loving nature. He prayed, as we must, with faith in a living God. . . . The Father and His Beloved Son appeared to Joseph in answer to his prayer. And he was told how to act, as he had desired. He obeyed like a child. He was told to join none of the churches. He did as he was told. And *because of his faithfulness, in the days and months and years ahead his prayers were answered with a flood of light and truth.*"[5]

> "The path to that in-person visitation of the Father and the Son began with a prompting from the Holy Ghost to pray."
> —Elder Robert D. Hales

Every Latter-day Saint and many people not of our faith who are somewhat familiar with our beginnings can answer the question, "Why did Joseph enter the grove of trees near his father's farm?" At least nine people out of ten will answer that he did so "because he wanted to know which church he should join." And that reply is perfectly correct. The Prophet himself explained, "My object in going to inquire of the Lord was to know which of all the sects was right, that I might know which to join" (Joseph Smith–History 1:18). Because Christianity is intended to be lived out in community, the church, or "body of Christ" (see Galatians 12:12, 27), to which one belongs is crucial.

But there was another reason why Joseph knelt in the Sacred Grove, a very personal, important one: he was concerned for the welfare of his own soul. In his earliest account of the First Vision (1832), Joseph recorded that "at about the age of twelve years my mind became seriously impressed with regard to the all-important concerns for the welfare of my immortal soul, which led me to searching the scriptures. . . . My mind became exceedingly distressed, for I became convicted of my sins." Historian Steven C. Harper wrote that "as Joseph realized the implication of the invitation to ask of God, his outlook changed completely. He had been scouring the Bible for the answer to his question, looking for a passage that would tell him where to find forgiveness. But then he experienced what he called 'a realising sense' that the Bible was less an archive of answers than it was a book of examples of people who asked for and received answers directly from God. This realization was part of Joseph's revelatory process."[6]

Later in that same 1832 account Joseph stated that "a pillar of light above the brightness of the sun at noon day came down from above and rested upon me, and I was filled with the Spirit of God, and the Lord opened the heavens upon me, and I saw the Lord, and he spake unto me, saying: *'Joseph, my son, thy sins are forgiven thee. Go thy way, walk in my statutes, and keep my commandments'*" (emphasis added).

Turning to Joseph's 1835 account, we read, "Being wrought up in my mind respecting the subject of religion, and looking at the different systems taught, I knew not who was right or who was wrong, and I considered it of the first importance that I should be right, in matters that involve eternal consequences." Later in this same account we read, "A pillar of fire appeared above my head. It presently rested down upon me and filled me with joy unspeakable. A personage appeared in the midst of this pillar of flame which was spread all around, and yet nothing consumed. Another personage soon appeared, like unto the first. *He said unto me, 'Thy sins are forgiven thee.'* He testified unto me that Jesus Christ is the Son of God" (emphasis added). That is also mentioned in Orson Pratt's 1840 account.

In a revelation given to the Prophet Joseph Smith at the time of the organization of the restored Church, Jesus Christ spoke of the coming of Moroni. But before detailing what Moroni did, the Lord said, "After it was truly manifested unto this first elder *that he had received a remission of his sins*, he was entangled again in the vanities of the world" (Doctrine and Covenants 20:5; emphasis added). This statement can only have reference to what took place in the First Vision, as set forth in the 1832, 1835, and 1840 (Pratt) accounts.

One other important point. Brother Joseph points out in his 1838 account: "It was on the morning of a beautiful, clear day, early in the spring of eighteen hundred and twenty. It was the first time in my life that I had made such an attempt, for amidst all my anxieties *I had never as yet made the attempt to pray vocally*" (Joseph Smith–History 1:14; emphasis added). My own experience teaches me that there is something special about a prayer spoken aloud, in which individuals express themselves freely and openly to their Father in Heaven. In addition, great blessings can flow as we prepare ourselves to pray, whether that be scripture reading, listening to uplifting music, meditation, and perhaps setting aside a specific time and place. Elder Neil L. Andersen wrote that "we show our Heavenly Father our true intent as we anticipate and plan for our communication with Him. Of course, many times our expressions are spontaneous, but when we set aside an important time and an important place, as we pray vocally with true intent, the power of our prayers ascends to heaven."[7]

JOSEPH'S WRESTLE WITH SATAN

It would be foolish and naïve to suppose that Lucifer, that son of the morning, the father of all lies (2 Nephi 2:18; Doctrine and Covenants 76:26), would stand by quietly while the marvelous work and a wonder was beginning to unfold. While we cannot read Satan's mind, it seems reasonable to suppose that he would do all in his power—and make no mistake about it, he is a being of great power—to block or stifle what was about to take place. It's as if he were saying, to use today's jargon, "I had better nip this in the bud!"[8] We would presume that Lucifer, whose knowledge and memory of our premortal existence is not veiled, would have known Joseph Smith Jr., one of the noble and great ones (see Abraham 3:22–23).

Joseph knelt in prayer as a seeker—in this case, seeking a remission of sins as well as an answer regarding which church he should join. From the official (1838) account, we read: "I had scarcely done so, when immediately I was seized upon by some power which entirely overcame me, and had such an astonishing influence over me as to bind my tongue so that I could not speak. Thick darkness gathered around me, and it seemed to me for a time as if I were doomed to sudden destruction." He adds that "at the very moment when I was ready to sink into despair and abandon myself to destruction—not to an imaginary ruin, but to *the power of some actual being from the unseen world, who had such marvelous power as I had never before felt in any being*—just at this moment of great alarm, I saw a pillar of light" (Joseph Smith–History 1:15–16; emphasis added).

The other primary First Vision account dictated by Joseph that mentions Satan's full-scale attack is the 1835 account. "Information was what I most desired at this time," Joseph explained, "and with a fixed determination to obtain it, I called upon the Lord for the first time, in the place above stated. Or, in other words, I made a fruitless attempt to pray. My tongue seemed to be swollen in my mouth,[9] so that I could not utter. I heard a noise behind me like someone walking towards me. I strove again to pray but could not. The noise of walking seemed to draw nearer. I sprang upon my feet and looked around but saw no person or thing that was calculated to produce the noise of walking."[10] Joseph's mention of hearing what sounded like someone approaching him is an example of a detail that would probably not be mentioned if the story were fabricated. That is especially true since nothing more is mentioned of whoever it was that walked toward him. While we do not know definitely what caused the sound of walking, could it not have been Satan himself, doing battle with the fourteen-year-old boy?

Orson Pratt's 1840 account describes the experience as follows: "At first, *he was severely tempted by the powers of darkness*, which endeavored to overcome him; but he continued to seek for deliverance, until darkness gave way from his mind; and he was enabled to pray in fervency of the spirit, and in faith" (emphasis added). One definition of *tempt* in Webster's 1828 *American Dictionary of the English Language* is "to put to trial"; another is "to provoke." In that sense, Joseph was tried severely, a trial that was not like anything most mortals will ever undergo. Meanings for *provoke* include "to challenge." Well, Satan certainly challenged the young prophet, a provocation so intense and overwhelming that Joseph feared he would die.

In Orson Hyde's 1842 account, we read that Joseph "began to pour out to the Lord, with fervent determination, the earnest desires of his soul. On one occasion, he went to a small grove of trees near his father's home and knelt down before God in solemn prayer. The adversary then made *several strenuous efforts to cool his ardent soul*. He filled his mind with doubts and brought to mind all manner of inappropriate images to prevent him from obtaining the object of his endeavors."[11] Elder Hyde described three specific satanic efforts. The first is that Satan "sought to cool his ardent soul." That is, the devil attempted to quench the fire of faith and trust in James's promise that God will honor an earnest request to know things of the Spirit (James 1:5–6). Second, according to Elder Hyde, Satan filled the boy's mind with doubt, which of course is antithetical to faith.[12] Third, Joseph was tempted to harbor "inappropriate images," perhaps immoral images, which, if not quickly dismissed, cause one to lose the Spirit (Doctrine and Covenants 42:23).

Having sung with a congregation of Saints the hymn "Joseph Smith's First Prayer," Elder Marion D. Hanks remarked: "This moving song has verses that start out with a lovely morning, things seeming good, bees humming, birds singing, music ringing through a grove; and with a boy undertaking to talk to God, shyly, without any experience but with great need. I was particularly struck by this thought when the lines you know were sung very well, but I wonder if you have heard them lately. 'When the powers of sin assailing filled his soul with deep despair.'"

Elder Hanks went on to remind us that "at the high times, the high moments, the pleasant, satisfying, sweet personally happy times—we are yet aware that . . . whether we like it or not, or whether we are ready or not, they are going to be making the effort. . . . There are powers that assail us, and when they do they fill our souls with deep despair. All of us have felt that, haven't we? Do you remember the words of the line following the one I quoted? 'But undaunted still he trusted in his Heavenly Father's care.' It didn't say that because we are nice people or we want to do the right thing either Joseph Smith or we would be immune from the powers that assail. *The promise for us and for him is confirmed in his account—that because he continued to trust even when his soul was filled with deep despair something happened and the something was a brilliant light which descended and dispersed the darkness that had gathered around him.*"[13] It is important for us to remember also that each account that mentions Joseph's wrestle with the evil one also states that the boy was delivered from the diabolical grasp by his strenuous efforts to pray, followed by the appearance of the Father and the Son.

• • •

Recently while reflecting on the First Vision and Satan's attack on the boy prophet, it occurred to me that there are other illustrations of this same phenomenon—that is, evil efforts to prevent spiritually significant events from taking place. My first thought was of the occasion when Moses was taken up into a high mountain, where he saw in vision the worlds that God had created, the multitudes of the children of God that would dwell on those worlds, and where he learned of the overall mission and purpose of the Father, the Son, and the Holy Ghost—"to bring to pass the immortality and eternal life of man" (Moses 1:39).

That occasion was after Moses beheld the burning bush and heard the voice of Jehovah but before Moses left to free the Israelite slaves from Egyptian bondage (Moses 1:17, 26). And of course, he was confronted by Satan. The father of lies sought to confuse or tempt the man who would, through divine empowerment, become the great Lawgiver. He insisted that Moses worship him as the Only Begotten Son of God. After three unsuccessful attempts to cast Satan out of his presence, Moses finally commanded him, in the name of the true Only Begotten, to depart, and he did so (Moses 1:19–21). Keep in mind that this was just prior to Moses encountering Pharaoh and miraculously leading the Israelites out of Egypt.

> "The nearer a person approaches the Lord, a greater power will be manifested by the adversary to prevent the accomplishment of His purposes."
> —Joseph Smith

Some fourteen hundred years later, Jesus Christ the Savior would be confronted by that same evil being, tempting the Lord by promising him the kingdoms of the world and the praise of masses of people. Jesus overcame Satan's taunts and temptations by quoting from the Old Testament (Deuteronomy 6:16; 8:3; Psalm 91:11–12). Note that this event took place just as Jesus was about to begin his ministry (JST, Matthew 4:1–11).

Another episode in our Church's history illustrates that same tactic—Satan's seeking to prevent a great work before it gets started. In this case, in 1837 Elders Heber C. Kimball, Orson Hyde, and some of their missionary associates had travelled to England to spread the glad tidings of the restored gospel. It was the night before the first baptisms in the British Isles were to take place in the River Ribble in Preston. Heber C. Kimball and Orson Hyde were attacked by a horde of evil spirits for an extended period of time. Heber later discussed this frightful experience with the Prophet Joseph, troubled that perhaps he and his brethren had done something wrong. "No, Brother Heber," Joseph replied, "at that time you were nigh unto the Lord; there was only a veil between you and Him, but you could not see Him. When I heard of it, it gave me great joy, for I then knew that the work of God had taken root in that land. It was this that caused the devil to make a struggle to kill you." The Prophet then explained some of his own battles with evil and remarked: "The nearer a person approaches the Lord, a greater power will be manifested by the adversary to prevent the accomplishment of His purposes."[14] It has ever been so, and we would expect no less than a full-scale attack on the one chosen to begin the final gospel dispensation.

Chapter 4

THE APPEARANCE

*I*n order for any person to come into the presence of God, he or she must be changed, spiritually lifted, transfigured. As it was when Moses received his glorious vision on an unnamed mountain (Moses 1:11, 14); when Peter, James, and John were with Jesus Christ on the Mount of Transfiguration (Matthew 17:1–9); and when the Three Nephite disciples were "sanctified in the flesh, that they were holy" (3 Nephi 28:39; see also 3 Nephi 28:6–9, 12–17, 30, 36–40), so fourteen-year-old Joseph Smith was *transfigured* in order to be able to remain in God's presence. "Transfiguration is the process by which a person is raised temporarily to a higher spiritual plane in order to be able to abide an intense spiritual presence or environment. . . . To be transfigured in this sense is to be infused with an added measure of divine strength and power."[1] Moses observed: "But now mine own eyes have beheld God; but not my natural, but my spiritual eyes, for my natural eyes could not have beheld; for I should have withered and died in his presence; but his glory was

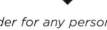

> In order for any person to come into the presence of God, he or she must be changed, spiritually lifted, transfigured. . . . Fourteen-year-old Joseph Smith was transfigured in order to be able to remain in God's presence.

upon me; and I beheld his face, for I was transfigured before him" (Moses 1:11).

President Russell M. Nelson taught: "Actually, the fact that the Father and the Son appeared to an untitled youth is one of the most remarkable aspects of the Restoration. Joseph Smith did not have to 'unlearn' anything. He was tutored personally by Them. Joseph was also tutored by other heavenly messengers. . . . His mission in mortality was foreordained. His receptive and pristine mind was open to the Lord's instruction. But, by worldly standards, Joseph was most unlikely. And his task to be the Prophet of this last dispensation seemed totally impossible. . . . This pattern is one the Lord has used repeatedly throughout history."[2]

BEINGS OF GLORY

When young Joseph was released from Satan's evil power and was able to continue his supplication to God, he experienced the glory and power and majesty of the first two members of the Godhead. How does one describe, explain, elucidate what it means to be brought into the immediate presence of resurrected, glorified beings? How do we, with our limited intellectual and spiritual capacity, speak of the power and glory that emanate from exalted personages? Jehovah used such words as the "devouring fire" or "everlasting burnings" to speak of what it will be like to live forever in celestial glory. In his official account (1838), Joseph Smith used "pillar of light" and "above the brightness of the sun" and "whose brightness and glory defy all description." In the 1835 account he used "a pillar of fire" and "pillar of flame." The account in the Wentworth letter (1842) speaks of "a

> How does one describe, explain, elucidate what it means to be brought into the immediate presence of resurrected, glorified beings? How do we, with our limited intellectual and spiritual capacity, speak of the power and glory that emanate from exalted personages?

brilliant light which eclipsed the sun at noon-day." All of this recalls for me how in Nauvoo the Prophet spoke often of the glory of God. Less than two months before his death, Joseph taught that "God Almighty Himself dwells in eternal fire. . . . Our God is a consuming fire."[3]

In Orson Pratt's 1840 account, we read that "as [the light] drew nearer, it increased in brightness, and magnitude, so that, by the time it reached the tops of the trees, the whole wilderness, for some distance around, was illuminated in a most glorious and brilliant manner. *He expected to have seen the leaves and boughs of the trees consumed, as soon as the light came in contact with them*; but, perceiving that it did not produce that effect, he was encouraged with the hopes of being able to endure its presence."[4]

ONE APPEARS, THEN ANOTHER

The Prophet's description of the descent of the two glorious personages is fascinating. In the 1835 account, Joseph commented that "a personage appeared in the midst of this pillar of flame which was spread all around, and yet nothing consumed. *Another personage soon appeared, like unto the first*."[5] According to David Nye White, Joseph explained that "directly I saw a light, and then a glorious personage in the light, *and then another personage* and the first personage said to the second, 'Behold, my beloved Son, hear him.'"[6]

It is worth noting that two of the accounts of the Vision (Joseph's 1835 account and David Nye White's 1843 account) speak of one personage appearing, *followed by the appearance of the second*. If we were to consider this matter in terms of priesthood government and order, I would suggest that God the Father appeared first, followed thereafter by Jesus Christ the Son.[7] On one occasion, Joseph taught that it is "the province of the Father to preside as the Chief or President, Jesus as the Mediator, and the Holy Ghost as the Testator or Witness."[8]

Reason with me on this matter, if you will. From David Nye White's account we read: "Directly I saw a light, and then a glorious personage in the light, and then another personage. *The first personage said to* [about] *the second, 'Behold my beloved Son. Hear him.'"* In Joseph's 1832 account, we read the following: "The Lord opened the heavens upon me and I saw the Lord and he spake unto me, saying, 'Joseph, my son, thy sins are forgiven thee. Go thy way, walk in my statutes, and keep my commandments. Behold, *I am the Lord of glory. I was crucified for the world that all those who believe on my name may have eternal life.'"*[9] It is clear in this latter statement that Jesus Christ is speaking.

"I SAW THE LORD"

One issue that has been raised is that in the 1832 account, Joseph states, "I was filled with the Spirit of God, and the Lord opened the heavens upon me, and *I saw the Lord*, and he spake unto me, saying, 'Joseph, my son, thy sins are forgiven thee.'"[10] The question that arises is, why in this earliest account does it state simply that "the Lord" appeared? Was there just one Being there? Some go so far as to suggest that in the years following the 1832 account Joseph sought to embellish or expand upon what he had said in the earliest account by adding a member of the Godhead to the vision.

In pondering this issue, I was reminded how frequently we speak in almost the broadest of terms when we speak of receiving divine assistance or blessings. Reflect on how often you have heard someone remark, "It's been a wonderful week. The Lord has really blessed me." Or, "I am striving to live in a manner that would please the Lord." When I say "the Lord blessed me," to whom am I referring? When I refer to pleasing the Lord, am I singling out Jesus or the Father? Which member of the Godhead do I have in mind? Is it the Father, or is it the Son? In saying that "the Lord blessed me," I am not trying to tease apart the holy Godhead, suggesting that the first member blesses me sometimes and the second sends me help occasionally. When I speak of "the Lord," I mean divine direction or strength or healing that come to me from Deity, from God.

It is worth noting that in January 1880 President John Taylor said, "*The Lord* appeared unto Joseph Smith, *both the Father and the Son*."[11] This would be no different from a Latter-day Saint speaking of the First Vision to a person of another faith and saying, "We believe that the heavens were opened in the spring of 1820 and that God appeared to Joseph Smith." People in Joseph's day used the words *Lord* and *God* interchangeably, just as we do today. In the early nineteenth century, *Lord* meant simply the Supreme Being.[12]

Look carefully at the following scriptural passages:

"The Lord giveth no commandments unto the children of men, save he shall prepare a way for them that they may accomplish the thing which he commandeth them" (1 Nephi 3:7).

"The Lord slayeth the wicked to bring forth his righteous purposes" (1 Nephi 4:13).

"Ye have forgotten what great things the Lord hath done for us" (1 Nephi 7:11).

"Six hundred years from the time that my father left Jerusalem, a prophet would the Lord God raise up among the Jews—even a Messiah, or, in other words, a Savior of the world" (1 Nephi 10:4).

"The Lord God will disperse the powers of darkness from before you" (Doctrine and Covenants 21:6).

"Thou shalt love the Lord thy God with all thy heart" (Doctrine and Covenants 59:5).

"Be thou humble; and the Lord thy God shall lead thee by the hand, and give thee answer to thy prayers" (Doctrine and Covenants 112:10).

"Now the Lord had shown unto me, Abraham, the intelligences that were organized before the world was" (Abraham 3:22).

Can you tell with certainty which God is being referred to in those passages—God the Father or God the Son? In a devotional address delivered to students at Brigham Young University, Elder Bruce R. McConkie provided valuable insight when he stated: "Be it remembered that most scriptures that speak of God or of the Lord do not even bother to distinguish the Father from the Son, simply because it doesn't make any difference which God is involved. They are one. The words or deeds of either of them would be the words and deeds of the other in the same circumstance.

> "Most scriptures that speak of God or of the Lord do not even bother to distinguish the Father from the Son, simply because it doesn't make any difference which God is involved. They are one. The words or deeds of either of them would be the words and deeds of the other in the same circumstance."
> —Elder Bruce R. McConkie

"Further, if a revelation comes from or by the power of the Holy Ghost, ordinarily the words will be those of the Son, though what the Son says will be what the Father would say, and the words may thus be considered as the Father's."[13]

WHAT DID THEY LOOK LIKE?

Four of the First Vision accounts make reference to the physical appearance of the first and second members of the Godhead. In his 1842 account (the Wentworth letter), as well as the 1840 account by Orson Pratt, the Prophet stated that he was "enwrapped in a heavenly vision and saw *two glorious personages who exactly resembled each other in their features and likeness.*" Orson Hyde's 1842 account states that "two glorious heavenly personages stood before him, *resembling each other exactly in features and stature.*" Alexander Neibaur's 1844 account states that young Joseph "saw a fire towards heaven come nearer and nearer. He saw a personage in the fire [who had a] *light complexion, blue eyes,* and a piece of white cloth drawn over his shoulders. His right arm [was] bare."[14]

A BROADENED PERSPECTIVE

Some years ago I took from the bookshelf in my office one of the journals I had kept during the administration of President Spencer W. Kimball. While browsing, I came across my written description of an experience I had while serving in a stake presidency in Florida. I reread with great satisfaction my account of one of the most noteworthy spiritual experiences in my life. Many of the same sweet feelings I felt at the time of the experience came back to me, and it was as if I were experiencing again the event some forty years later.

As I read through what I had written then, however, I found myself saying aloud, "Yes, that's basically what happened, but it would be more accurate to say _____." Consequently, I found myself lining out some of what I had written earlier and rewriting above the line a few of the sentences in the journal, not contradicting what I had written earlier, but instead clarifying or making plainer what had been written. Why was I able to do this? Simply because decades had passed, and I had matured in my thinking and my manner of expression. The reality of the experience was not in question at all. I knew it, and, as Joseph Smith would have said, I knew that God knew it (see Joseph Smith–History 1:25). As a result of scores of experiences I had had through the years—both good and bad, pleasurable as well as painful—my spiritual perspective had broadened, my abilities as a writer had been refined, and I could now view that particular experience with new eyes. I could also write of it with greater clarity and even greater accuracy.

So it was with the Prophet Joseph. The First Vision took place in 1820, and the initial effort to record that theophany occurred twelve years later, in the year 1832. During those years, Joseph had been visited by Moroni, John the Baptist, and Peter, James, and John; grieved at the death of his brother Alvin; been married to Emma Hale; received and translated what was engraved on the gold plates and carried out the publication of the Book of Mormon; organized, under the direction of the Lord, the restored Church; established the law of consecration and stewardship among the Saints; learned of and visited Independence, Missouri, the future site of the New Jerusalem; received and recorded more than seventy revelations that are now found in the Doctrine and Covenants; been engaged in his inspired translation of the Bible for two years; and received the vision of the three degrees of glory (Doctrine and Covenants 76).

How could anyone be the same after such marvelous and magnificent and mind-expanding experiences as Joseph had during those twelve years? Is it so strange, or should it be troublesome, then, to discover that the 1835, 1838, and 1842 reports of the vision in Palmyra should be rendered differently? He could certainly see and understand and report on the First Vision with a broadened, increasingly mature perspective on what actually took place.

BIBLICAL PARALLELS

Not long ago I was visited by a minister of another faith whom I had never met. He indicated that he had a few questions he wanted to pose to me. Sadly, most of them were of the baiting kind, what I sometimes refer to as "gotcha" inquiries. That is, the person was not really asking an information-seeking question. He pointed out to me (just in case I didn't already know this) that there are differences in detail among the various accounts of the First Vision.

I looked at him, smiled, and then said, "Do you really want to go there?"

He responded with, "What do you mean?"

I told him that my response to his query would take him where he probably did not want to go. He insisted, however, that he wanted an answer.

I stated, "Your critique of the First Vision could also be leveled at the Bible. How do you explain the differences between many parallel passages in the New Testament, particularly the four Gospels?" For example, I pointed out, Matthew and Luke cannot get together on

Jesus's genealogy (Matthew 1:1–16; Luke 3:23–38). Such important events as the visit of the wise men and the special star that guided them when Jesus was at least two years old, as recorded by Matthew, are not even alluded to in the other three Gospels (Matthew 2:1–11). Matthew and Mark speak of Jesus feeding two multitudes, one group of five thousand and another of four thousand (Matthew 14:14–21; Mark 6:33–34; 8:1–9), whereas Luke and John mention only the feeding of five thousand (Luke 9:11–17; John 6:5–14). Matthew and Mark agree that on Resurrection morning one angel appeared outside the Garden Tomb to the Lord's disciples (Matthew 28:2; Mark 16:5); Luke indicates that there were two (Luke 24:4); John does not mention any angels at all (John 20:1–10). John wrote that the first person to see the risen Lord was Mary Magdalene, who was alone on that occasion (John 20:1–9), and yet Matthew speaks of a group of women disciples, including Mary Magdalene, seeing the Lord soon after he had come out of the tomb (Matthew 28:1–9).

I pointed out that we find exactly the same thing in the Acts of the Apostles. For example, we can detect slight differences in detail surrounding Paul's conversion, as given in chapters 9, 22, and 26. In Acts 9, Luke describes Paul's encounter with the risen Lord on the road to Damascus (Acts 9:1–20); in chapter 22 we read of Paul's defense before a crowd of angry Jewish leaders (Acts 22:1–28); and in chapter 26 we find the magnificent description of Paul's defense before King Agrippa II while Paul was imprisoned at Caesarea (Acts 26:1–29). In Acts 9 Paul is struck down. "And the men which journeyed with him stood speechless, hearing a voice, but seeing no man" (v. 7). In Acts 22, Luke records Paul's saying, "They that were with me saw indeed the light, and were afraid; but they heard not the voice of him that spake to me" (v. 9). And in Acts 26 (Paul's defense before Agrippa), Paul explains that he and the members of his company were struck down and that he heard the voice of the Lord Jesus Christ. Nothing is mentioned regarding what the other men saw or heard.

Which is it? Did Paul's fellow travelers hear the Savior's voice, or did they not? Now, my experience teaches me that very few Christians would be troubled enough about the inconsistences in the Gospels and in Luke's account of Paul's conversion to be shaken in their beliefs, to have a major faith crisis, to threaten to walk away from their Christian way of life because of those inconsistencies. Why then should those same people expect that thinking and committed Latter-day Saints would be distressed to learn that there are slight differences in Joseph Smith's four accounts of his vision in the Sacred Grove?

We need to appreciate that each of the accounts was written to a different audience for a different purpose. In his groundbreaking book, *Joseph Smith's First Vision*, first published in 1971, historian Milton V. Backman Jr. explained: "Some have suggested that if a person does not relate an experience in the same manner each time he discusses the event, then he is not to be considered a reliable witness. In an important way, however, the fact that the four recitals of the First Vision are different helps support the integrity of the Mormon Prophet. The variations indicate that Joseph Smith did not deliberately create a memorized version which he related to everyone. . . . While the wordings in Joseph's account are different, a number of basic truths are disclosed in each of his recitals, clearly indicating a rich harmony in many details."[15]

> "The fact that the four recitals of the First Vision are different helps support the integrity of the Mormon Prophet. The variations indicate that Joseph Smith did not deliberately create a memorized version which he related to everyone. . . . While the wordings in Joseph's account are different, a number of basic truths are disclosed in each of his recitals, clearly indicating a rich harmony in many details."
> —Milton V. Backman

In addressing BYU students in a devotional assembly, Professor Richard Lloyd Anderson noted: "Critics love to dwell on supposed inconsistencies in Joseph Smith's spontaneous accounts of his first vision. But people normally give shorter and longer accounts of a vivid experience that is retold more than once. . . . Thus his most detailed first vision account [1838] came after several others—at the time that he began his formal history that he saw as one of the key responsibilities of his life (see [Joseph Smith–History] 1:1–2, 17–20). In Paul's case there is the parallel. His most detailed account of Christ's call is the last recorded mention of several. Thus before Agrippa, Paul related how the glorified Savior first prophesied his [Paul's] work among the gentiles; this was told only then because Paul was speaking before a gentile audience (see Acts 26:16–18). Paul and Joseph Smith had reasons for delaying full details of their visions until the proper time and place."[16]

> "One historian who does not believe Joseph Smith said that he couldn't trust the accounts of the vision because they were subjective and that it was his job to figure out what really happened. But how will this skeptical scholar discover what actually happened when he is unwilling to trust the only eyewitness or the process of personal revelation? Such historians assume godlike abilities to know, yet they don't trust God's ability to reveal truth or theirs to receive it."
>
> —Steven C. Harper

Historian Steven C. Harper emphasized that "it is not wise to take for granted that Joseph Smith's memory was accurate at the time of his experience but increasingly inaccurate in proportion to the passage of time. Nor is it wise to assume that his memories were inaccurate because they contain discrepancies. . . . Joseph Smith's memories reflect his growing awareness of the vision's meaning."[17]

I suppose there will always be those in our society who will not accept any of the accounts of the First Vision because such persons do not (or will not) yield to the possibility that such a thing could happen. Harper continued: "One historian who does not believe Joseph Smith said that he couldn't trust the accounts of the vision because they were subjective and that it was his job to figure out what really happened. But how will this skeptical scholar discover what actually happened when he is unwilling to trust the only eyewitness or the process of personal revelation? Such historians assume godlike abilities to know, yet they don't trust God's ability to reveal truth or theirs to receive it. They don't seem to grasp the profound irony that *they are replacing the subjectivity of historical witnesses with their own.* I call their method subjectivity squared. They dismiss the historical documents and severely limit possible interpretations by predetermining that Joseph's story is not credible."[18]

THE FATHER TESTIFIES OF THE SON

President Joseph Fielding Smith taught an important principle when he explained that "all revelation since the fall has come through Jesus Christ, who is the Jehovah of the Old Testament. In all of the scriptures, where God is mentioned and where he has appeared, it was Jehovah who talked with Abraham, with Noah, Enoch, Moses and all the prophets. He is the God of Israel, the Holy One of Israel. . . . The Father has never dealt directly and personally since the fall, and he has never appeared except to introduce and bear record of the Son."[19] Elsewhere President Smith pointed out that "after Adam's transgression he was shut out of the presence of the Father who has remained hidden from his children to this day, with a few exceptions wherein righteous men have been privileged with the glorious privilege of seeing him. . . . Since the fall all revelation and commandments from the Father have come through Jesus Christ."[20]

That principle is borne out in two corrections that the Prophet Joseph Smith made in his inspired translation of the Bible. In the King James Version, John 1:18 reads, "No man has seen God at any time," but the Joseph Smith Translation reads, "No man hath seen God at any time, *except he hath borne record of the Son*; for except it is through him no man can be saved" (JST, John 1:19; emphasis added). Similarly, in the King James Version, 1 John 4:12 states, "No man hath seen God at any time," whereas the Joseph Smith Translation renders the passage as "No man hath seen God at any time, *except them who believe*" (emphasis added; see also KJV, 3 John 1:11).

I have purposely taken the time to make this point, primarily so that we can come to appreciate just how singularly significant Joseph Smith's First Vision was. In the words of Elder John A. Widtsoe, "It was an extraordinary experience. Never before had God the Father and God the Son appeared to mortal man."[21] We are aware of several occasions when the voice of God the Father has been heard as the Father bore witness of the Son. Some of these include at the baptism of Jesus (Matthew 3:17; Mark 1:11; Luke 3:22); after the Savior's triumphal entry (John 12:28); on the Mount of Transfiguration (Matthew 17:5; Mark 9:7; Luke 9:35); and when the risen Lord appears to his ancient American Saints (3 Nephi 11:7). We know that Stephen the martyr saw a vision of Christ standing on the right hand of the Father (Acts 7:55). But the times when the Father and the Son have appeared together to mortal men or women are extremely rare.

The very act of the Father introducing the Son is a great lesson, a primer of the principle that God's house is a house of order, a tutorial in priesthood government. President Joseph Fielding Smith put it this way: "We have a wonderful illustration of how revelation comes through Christ presented to us in the Vision given to the Prophet Joseph Smith. . . .

"Had Joseph Smith come home from the grove and declared that the Father and the Son appeared to him and that the Father spoke to him and answered his question while the Son stood silently by, then we could have [identified] the story as a fraud. Joseph Smith was too young and inexperienced to know this at the time, but he made no mistake, and his story was in perfect harmony with divine truth, with the divine law that Christ is the Mediator between God and man."[22]

One other matter. In the 1835 account, we read the following: "He

[Christ] said unto me, 'Thy sins are forgiven thee.' He testified that Jesus Christ is the Son of God. *I saw many angels in this vision.*"[23] No other contemporary account mentions the appearance of angels. But should such a thing surprise us? Keeping in mind that the implications of this singular visionary experience were absolutely earth-shaking, that the long night of darkness when the fulness of the gospel was not on earth was coming to an end, that angel after angel would appear to Joseph Smith and his co-laborers in the restored gospel to respond to questions, instruct, confer, and ordain—it would not be out of the ordinary to learn that other heavenly messengers would be in attendance to witness the greatest event in the history of the world since the Resurrection of Jesus Christ. Frankly, "there is no reason to suppose that when Joseph says, 'I saw two personages,' he means that he saw them at exactly the same time for precisely the same length of time or that he did not see others besides the two."[24] It was a day of rejoicing, a time when the heavens resounded.

Brigham Young University professor Truman G. Madsen wisely observed: "Some critics have pointed out that the Prophet spoke of the visit of angels in connection with his first vision. Some have theorized that he began by asserting that he saw an angel and ended up embellishing it with the claim that he saw the Father and the Son. . . . It is an enforced either-or to say that he saw the Father and the Son or saw angels. What he saw was both."[25]

• • •

Our Heavenly Father and the Lord Jesus Christ chose to open the heavens by calling an unsophisticated but receptive and spiritually sensitive youth. Elder Orson Pratt put it well when he declared that Joseph Smith was "uncontaminated by [old Christian] traditions, as he was not a member of any church. . . . He was uneducated; he had not been to college; he was not trained in the vices of all large cities; but merely a country boy accustomed to hard work with his father."²⁶ God could mold and shape the mind and heart of such a pure and receptive youth.

"Joseph Smith's 19th-century frontier environment was aflame with competing crowds of Christian witnesses," Elder Jeffrey R. Holland observed. "But in the tumult they created, these exuberant revivalists were, ironically, obscuring the very Savior young Joseph so earnestly sought. Battling what he called 'darkness and confusion,' he retreated to the solitude of a grove of trees where he saw and heard a more glorious witness of the Savior's centrality to the gospel. . . . With a gift of sight unimagined and unanticipated, Joseph beheld in vision his Heavenly Father, the great God of the universe, and Jesus Christ, His perfect Only Begotten Son. Then the Father set the example. . . . He pointed to Jesus, saying: 'This is My Beloved Son. Hear Him!' *No greater expression of Jesus's divine identity, His primacy in the plan of salvation, and His standing in the eyes of God could ever exceed that short seven-word declaration.*"²⁷

> "If every one of us knew in our hearts that [Joseph Smith's testimony of his vision] is true, then we would know that all else which follows it, which came through the restoration of the gospel, is true also. And we would walk and live with greater faithfulness."
> —President Gordon B. Hinckley

The time had arrived for young Joseph Smith to begin his spiritual education, and the Gods of heaven chose to begin it by coming to earth and meeting with him in a private interview. "If every one of us knew in our hearts that [Joseph Smith's testimony of his vision] is true," President Gordon B. Hinckley taught, "then we would know that all else which follows it, which came through the restoration of the gospel, is true also. And we would walk and live with greater faithfulness."²⁸

Joseph would acquire light and truth "line upon line, precept upon precept" (2 Nephi 28:30) and would grow in spiritual stature a little at a time. Revelations would come. Angels would appear. Priesthoods would be restored. Temples would be erected. But first young Joseph needed to meet God face to face. The Gods of heaven needed to descend from their throne above. That took place in the spring of 1820. The prophetic word given to Enoch was in process of being fulfilled: "And righteousness will I send down out of heaven; and truth will I send forth out of the earth" (Moses 7:62; see also Psalm 85:11). Indeed, the ultimate Truth came down from heaven as embodied by the Father and the Son, truth that would set millions of people free (John 8:31–32)—free from superstition, free from falsehoods, free from ignorance.

Chapter 5

"THEIR HEARTS ARE FAR FROM ME"

We recall that the young prophet went into the grove for two reasons: first, he was concerned about his own eternal welfare and yearned for a remission of his sins. Second, he desperately needed an answer to a crucial question: With all the variant voices then being sounded in camp meetings and revivals, which voice should he believe? What Christian church should he join?"

JOSEPH POSES HIS QUESTION

One cannot imagine the impact such a heavenly phenomenon would have on the eyes, the heart, the mind, the soul. The magnificent power and glory attending the appearance of the Father and the Son would be ineffable; it would be something beyond description. We read in the account of the First Vision contained in the Wentworth letter (1842): "While fervently engaged in supplication, my mind was taken away from the objects with which I was surrounded, and I was enwrapped in a heavenly vision and saw two glorious personages who exactly resembled each other in features and likeness, surrounded with a brilliant light which eclipsed the sun at noon day."[1]

This grand and glorious encounter was no formalized administrative task. While it would obviously have implications that would reach to all the world and affect hundreds of millions of persons in the future, it was, first and foremost, a personal experience. In initiating the restitution of all things that would, as we have said, revolutionize the whole world, the Almighty took occasion to first call the fourteen-year-old boy by name. "One of them spake unto me, calling me by name" (Joseph Smith–History 1:18).[2] It was a tender and endearing moment. God the Father and his Son, Jesus Christ, knew this young man, indeed had known him for millennia, for Joseph was, in the language of Alma, "called and prepared from the foundation of the world according to the foreknowledge of God, on account of [his] exceeding faith and good works" in the premortal world (Alma 13:3).

A little more than two thousand years before Joseph's experience in the Sacred Grove, two decades before the birth of the Messiah, Jehovah had spoken gently and lovingly to Nephi, son of Helaman: "Behold, thou art Nephi, and I am God" (Helaman 10:6). In the meridian of time the Savior had at Caesarea Philippi stated to his chief apostle, "Thou art Peter" (Matthew 16:18). It matters a great deal to persons to hear someone speak their name, especially if that someone is God. The boy prophet "learned that a soul in the early nineteenth century was just as precious unto God as a soul in Moses' time or in the meridian of time, else why would the Lord answer his humble prayer and appear in person? Moreover, Joseph learned that personal revelation may be received by those who humble themselves and approach God with unwavering faith and with broken hearts and contrite spirits."[3]

In his first account of the vision (1832), Joseph recorded: "I saw the Lord, and he spake unto me, saying, 'Joseph my son, *thy sins are forgiven thee.* Go thy way, walk in my statutes, and keep my commandments.'"[4] Similarly, the 1835 account contains these words: "A personage appeared in the midst of this pillar of flame, which was spread all around and yet nothing consumed. Another personage soon appeared like unto the first. He said unto me, *'Thy sins are forgiven thee.'* He testified unto me that Jesus Christ is the Son of God."[5]

And so young Joseph's hope in calling upon the Lord in prayer in the first place—that is, seeking a remission of sins—was realized, for the young man could not have come into the divine presence without first being cleansed from sin (see Doctrine and Covenants 67:10). Indeed, the Saints have been promised that when their eyes are single to his glory, when their minds have been sanctified, their sins have been forsaken, and they strive thereafter to keep the commandments, they will see the Lord's face and know that he is (Doctrine and Covenants 88:67–68; 93:1).

THE UNEXPECTED ANSWER COMES

Joseph recorded: "My object in going to inquire of the Lord was to know which of all the sects was right, that I might know which to join" (Joseph Smith–History 1:18). It wasn't enough for Joseph to want to know which church was right. He wanted to know *which church he should join.* Joseph yearned to know something very important, so that he could *act upon* that knowledge. "The classic example of asking in faith," Elder David A. Bednar explained, "is Joseph Smith and the First Vision. As young Joseph was seeking to know the truth about religion, he read the following verse in the first chapter of James. . . . Please notice the requirement to ask in faith, which I understand to mean the necessity to not only express but to do, the dual obligation *to both plead and to perform,* the requirement *to communicate and to act.*

"Pondering this biblical text led Joseph to retire to a grove of trees near his home to pray and to seek spiritual knowledge. . . . Joseph's questions focused not just on what he needed to know but also on *what was to be done!* His prayer was not simply, 'Which church is right?' His

> *It wasn't enough for Joseph to want to know which church was right. He wanted to know which church he should join. Joseph yearned to know something very important, so that he could act upon that knowledge.*

question was, 'Which church should I join?' Joseph went to the grove to ask in faith, and he was determined to act."[6]

"No sooner, therefore, did I get possession of myself," Joseph continued, "so as to be able to speak, than I asked the Personages who stood above me in the light, which of all the sects was right, that I might know which to join." Then comes this important insight into Joseph's mind and heart: "For at this time it had never entered into my heart that all were wrong" (Joseph Smith–History 1:18). Some critics have been quick to point out that this latter expression—that it had never occurred to him that all of the churches were wrong—is at variance with what is contained in the 1832 account. In that earliest account we read the following:

- "They [the different denominations] did not adorn their profession by a holy walk and conversation."
- "Mankind did not come unto the Lord, but they had apostatized from the true and living faith, and there was no society or denomination that built upon the gospel of Jesus Christ, as recorded in the New Testament."
- "They have turned aside from the gospel and keep not my commandments."[7]

The answer here is to be found in the fact that the 1832 account is referring largely to *individual Christians* whose lives did not reflect the true Christian faith. Humankind had apostatized. And there was no society or denomination *with which Joseph was acquainted* that built upon the gospel of Jesus Christ as set forth in the New Testament. Joseph was here describing a tragic situation and making a painful acknowledgment. It's as if the young prophet was saying, sadly, "Surely the Lord's true church must be somewhere on this earth. I cannot imagine that it's not out there somewhere!"

The Savior employed strong language to express his disappointment, even his righteous indignation, regarding the state of the religious world: "I was answered that I must join none of them, for they were all wrong; and the Personage who addressed me said that all their creeds were an abomination in his sight; that those professors were all corrupt; that 'they draw near to me with their lips, but their hearts are far from me, they teach for doctrines the commandments of men, having a form of godliness, but they deny the power thereof'" (Joseph Smith–History 1:19).[8] So Joseph was instructed strongly that he should not join or affiliate with any denomination in the area, including Baptist, Methodist, Presbyterian, or Universalist.

> Joseph was instructed strongly that he should not join or affiliate with any denomination in the area, including Baptist, Methodist, Presbyterian, or Universalist.

WHAT WENT WRONG?

What exactly happened in Christian history and practice to bring about what Latter-day Saints refer to as a universal apostasy? Consider the following:

1. The early Christians were persecuted. Jesus himself warned his apostles, as they sat on the Mount of Olives, of the days to come: "Take heed that no man deceive you; for many shall come in my name, saying—I am Christ—and shall deceive many; *then shall they deliver you up to be afflicted, and shall kill you,* and ye shall be hated of all nations, for my name's sake" (Joseph Smith–Matthew 1:5–7; emphasis added; see also 1 Nephi 13:5–6).

Persecution first came from the Jews, who saw the followers of Jesus as apostates and traitors. The Romans later persecuted the early Saints, particularly during the reigns of such emperors as Nero (A.D. 54–68), Vespasian (A.D. 69–79), and Domitian (A.D. 81–96). And yet, it is important to clarify that Roman persecution was not the most significant element in the apostasy of the Christian church. As President David O. McKay pointed out, "inner weakness is more dangerous and more fatal than outward opposition. The Church is little if at all injured by persecution and calumnies from ignorant, misinformed, or malicious enemies; a greater hindrance to its progress comes from faultfinders, shirkers, commandment-breakers, and apostate cliques within."[9]

2. People from within the faith—whose commitment to the gospel had waned—fought against the Church. The apostle Paul spoke often of this very concern. In his farewell to the elders of the Church at Ephesus: "Take heed . . . unto yourselves, and to all the flock, over the which the Holy Ghost hath made you overseers, to feed the church of God, which he hath purchased with his own blood. For I know this, that after my departing shall grievous wolves enter in among you, not sparing the flock. Also of your own selves shall men arise, speaking perverse things, to draw away disciples after them" (Acts 20:28–30).

Paul warned Timothy that the Spirit had declared to him that "in the latter times some shall depart from the faith, giving heed to seducing spirits, and doctrines of devils; speaking lies in hypocrisy; having their conscience seared with a hot iron; forbidding to marry, and commanding to abstain from meats, which God hath created to be received with thanksgiving of them which believe and know the truth" (1 Timothy 4:1–3). In many ways, the apostasy of the Christian church was more of a mutiny, a revolt.

3. The ordinances of the early Church were altered, modified, twisted, and, in some cases, jettisoned. This is especially the case with regard to the blessing of babies, the mode of baptism, infant baptism, and the Sacrament of the Lord's Supper. Isaiah had prophesied of just such a time: "The earth also is defiled under the inhabitants thereof; because they have transgressed the laws, changed the ordinance, broken the everlasting covenant" (Isaiah 24:5). In describing the state of things at the opening of this dispensation, the Lord said specifically that "they have strayed from mine ordinances, and have broken mine everlasting covenant" (Doctrine and Covenants 1:15). Joseph Smith's mandate was clear: "Ordinances instituted in the heavens before the foundation of

the world, in the priesthood, for the salvation of men, are not to be altered or changed. All must be saved on the same principles."[10]

4. Plain and precious truths were taken away or kept back from the Bible (1 Nephi 13:20–40). Elder Orson Pratt observed that many of the differences between New Testament manuscripts from the third and fourth centuries "are of no particular consequence, as they do not materially alter the sense. But there are many thousands of differences wherein the sense is entirely altered. *How are translators to know which of the manuscripts, if any, contain the true sense? They have no original copies with which to compare them—no standard of correction.* No one can tell whether even one verse of either the Old or New Testament conveys the ideas of the original author."[11]

The Prophet Joseph thus declared: "I believe the Bible as it read when it came from the pen of the original writers. Ignorant translators, careless transcribers, or designing or corrupt priests have committed many errors."[12] The headnote to section 76 of the Doctrine and Covenants quotes from Joseph Smith's history: "From sundry revelations which had been received, it was apparent that many important points touching the salvation of man had been taken from the Bible, or lost before it was compiled."

That the Prophet should be "appointed" by God (Doctrine and Covenants 42:56; 76:15) and called to undertake a "new translation" of the Bible implies of itself that the Bible, though essentially true, needed clarification, correction, and supplementation at the hands of an inspired translator. Indeed, the early Latter-day Saints exulted in the fact that the Bible was "undergoing the purifying touch by a revelation of Jesus Christ."[13]

"In place of the 'plain and precious' doctrines of the gospel," Elder Neal A. Maxwell pointed out, "grew the stumbling blocks (1 Nephi 13:28), leaving inadequate explanations concerning, for example, the character of God and His purposes as well as the 'why' questions about human agency and suffering. The absence of plain and precious truths brings intellectual impasses and impediments to developing faith."[14]

5. A blending of Greek philosophy and Christian theology took place, resulting in the loss or corruption of significant doctrine. The following are examples of doctrines that were corrupted during the Apostasy but restored through the Prophet Joseph Smith:

> A blending of Greek philosophy and Christian theology took place, resulting in the loss or corruption of significant doctrine.

• The nature of God the Father. Modern prophets have declared that He is a personal Being; has a body of flesh and bones; is our Heavenly Father, the Father of our spirits; is a glorified, exalted personage, a Man of Holiness (Moses 6:57); is a Being who possesses all the powers and attributes of godliness but who is approachable, knowable, one who, like Christ, can be touched with the feeling of our infirmities (Hebrews 4:15).

• The gospel of Jesus Christ as a new and everlasting covenant. Scriptures of the Restoration reveal Christ's eternal gospel, the profound truth that Christian prophets have declared Christian doctrine and administered Christian ordinances since the days of Adam (see Doctrine and Covenants 49:9; 66:2). In speaking of biblical truths that have survived the removal of plain and precious things, Joseph Smith stated: "Now taking it for granted that the scriptures say what they mean, and mean what they say, we have sufficient grounds to go on and prove from the Bible that the gospel has always been the same; the ordinances to fulfill its requirements, the same, and the officers to officiate, the same; and the signs and fruits resulting from the promises, the same."[15]

• The relationship among the three members of the Godhead. Without apostolic oversight, the corruption of fundamental and foundational truths began to take place, such as the truth that the Father, the Son, and the Holy Ghost are three distinct beings, three Gods.

Joseph Smith spoke plainly: "I have always declared God to be a distinct personage, Jesus Christ a separate and distinct personage from God the Father, and that the Holy Ghost was a distinct personage and a Spirit: and these three constitute three personages and three Gods."[16]

President Dallin H. Oaks spoke of a blending of Greek philosophy with Christian theology: "We maintain that the concepts identified by such nonscriptural terms as 'the incomprehensible mystery of God' and 'the mystery of the Holy Trinity' are attributable to the ideas of Greek philosophy. These philosophical concepts transformed Christianity in the first few centuries following the deaths of the Apostles. For example, philosophers then maintained that physical matter was evil and that God was a spirit without feelings or passions."[17]

"We know the Apostasy occurred in part because the philosophies of men were elevated over Christ's basic, essential doctrine," Elder Quentin L. Cook taught. "Instead of the simplicity of the Savior's message being taught, many plain and precious truths were changed or lost. In fact, Christianity adopted some Greek philosophical traditions to reconcile people's beliefs with their existing culture. The historian Will Durant wrote: '*Christianity did not destroy paganism; it adopted it.*'"[18]

Think further upon what was lost, and thus what needed to be restored:

- The identity of Jesus Christ as Jehovah.
- The necessity of the ordinances of salvation, both the proper authority and the specific manner in which they are to be performed.
- The eternal significance of temples, temple ordinances, and sealing powers.
- We are literal, spirit children of God.
- The premortal existence of our spirits.
- The innocence and salvation of little children and the age of accountability.

- Life in the postmortal world of spirits and the work done there.
- Degrees of glory in the hereafter.
- The capacity of mortals to become, through the transforming power of Jesus Christ and the ordinances of salvation, even as God is.

Now, having considered what took place in early Christianity, we must remember that not all people—including church leaders—who lived during the years when the fulness of the gospel was not on the earth were corrupt, spiritually given over to Satan, and consumed with evil. "In our assertion that the Church had apostatized,"[19] Elder Alexander B. Morrison wrote, "we must *not* conclude that all virtue had left the world. We must *not* for even a moment think that with the apostasy a blanket of spiritual darkness, keeping out all light and truth, descended upon humankind, suffering and choking off every good and worthy thought and deed, erasing Christ from every heart. That just didn't happen, and we do a grave injustice to all Christians, including ourselves, if we think otherwise. Indeed, I think it true that, in some ways at least, mainstream Christian denominations are weaker *now*, after the Restoration, than the Church was three centuries after Christ."[20]

> "Christianity adopted some Greek philosophical traditions to reconcile people's beliefs with their existing culture. The historian Will Durant wrote: 'Christianity did not destroy paganism; it adopted it.'"
> —Elder Quentin L. Cook

"ONLY TRUE CHURCH": WHAT IT DOES NOT MEAN

"They were all wrong" (Joseph Smith–History 1:19). It isn't the case that everything the churches of that day taught and everything they did was wrong. No doubt there was much truth being declared and tremendous good being done. Rather, none of the churches on the earth at that time were His church, the Lord's Church, directed by apostles and prophets, with the fulness of the gospel. Not one denomination was built upon the foundation of apostles and prophets (Ephesians 2:19–20), and hence there were no "special witnesses of the name of Christ in all the world" (Doctrine and Covenants 107:23). They did not possess nor exercise apostolic priesthood authority, the power to bind on earth and have those actions sealed everlastingly in the heavens (Matthew 16:19; 18:18; Helaman 10:7; Doctrine and Covenants 128:9–11); there was no apostolic oversight to "build up the church and regulate all of the affairs of the same" (Doctrine and Covenants 107:33); there was no apostolic vision, and "where there is no vision, the people perish" (Proverbs 29:18); there were no anointed seers, chosen visionaries who see things "not visible to the natural eye" (Moses 6:36), men who are able to perceive and anticipate falsehood and distortion; there were none with anointed eyes to oversee the declaration and interpretation of doctrine, to insure that what people read and what they were taught was true.

"They were all wrong." That is essentially what the Lord states in the Preface to the Doctrine and Covenants when he refers to The Church of Jesus Christ of Latter-day Saints as "the only true and living church upon the face of the whole earth" (Doctrine and Covenants 1:30). Admittedly, this is strong language; it is hard doctrine, words that are hurtful and offensive to persons of other faiths. It may be helpful to consider briefly what the phrase "the only true and living church" means and what it does *not* mean. First, let's deal with what the phrase *does not* mean.

1. It does not mean that men and women of other Christian faiths are not sincere believers in biblical truth and genuine followers of Christ. Latter-day Saints have no difficulty whatsoever accepting a person's affirmation that they are Christian, that they acknowledge Jesus Christ as the divine Son of God, their Savior. Nor are Latter-day Saints the only ones entitled to inspiration or personal divine guidance for their lives.

2. It does not mean that others are worshipping "a different Jesus," as many in the Christian world often say of the Latter-day Saints today. Rather, we acknowledge that true Christians worship Jesus of Nazareth, the Son of God, the Promised Messiah.

3. It does not mean we believe that most of the doctrine in Catholic, Eastern Orthodox, or Protestant Christianity is false or that all of the leaders of the various branches of Christianity have improper motives. Joseph Smith stated: "The inquiry is frequently made of me, 'Wherein do you differ from others in your religious views?' In reality and essence we do not differ so far in our religious views, but that we could all drink into one principle of love. One of the grand fundamental principles of 'Mormonism' is to receive truth, let it come from whence it may."[21]

"Have the Presbyterians any truth?" he asked on another occasion. "Yes. Have the Baptists, Methodists, etc., any truth? Yes. They all have a little truth mixed with error. We should gather all the good and true principles in the world and treasure them up, or we shall not come out pure 'Mormons.'"[22] President George Albert Smith thus spoke lovingly to persons of other faiths by way of invitation: "We have come not to take away from you the truth and virtue you possess. We have come not to find fault with you nor to criticize you. We have not come here to berate you. . . . Keep all the good that you have, and *let us bring to you more good.*"[23]

Then what of the Latter-day Saint belief that plain and precious truths and many covenants of the Lord were removed from the Bible before its compilation? (1 Nephi 13:20–40; Moses 1:40–41).[24] Although, as we noted earlier, we do not subscribe to a doctrine of biblical sufficiency or inerrancy, we do believe that the hand of God has been over the preservation of the biblical materials, such that what we have now is what the Almighty would have us possess. In the words of Elder Bruce R. McConkie, delivered to religious educators, "we cannot avoid the conclusion that a divine providence is directing all things as they should be. This means that the Bible, as it now is, contains that portion of the Lord's word" that the present world is prepared to receive.[25] Indeed, although Latter-day Saints do not believe the Bible contains now all that it once contained, the Bible is a remarkable book of scripture, one that inspires, motivates, reproves, corrects, and instructs (see 2 Timothy 3:16). It is the word of God.[26]

4. It does not mean that God disapproves of or rejects all that devoted Christians are teaching or doing, where their heart is, and what they hope to accomplish in the religious world. "God, the Father of us all," President Ezra Taft Benson said, "uses the men of the earth, especially good men, to accomplish his purposes. It has been true in the past, it is true today, it will be true in the future." President Benson then quoted the following from a conference address delivered by Elder Orson F. Whitney in April 1928: "'Perhaps the Lord needs such men on the outside of His Church to help it along. They are among its auxiliaries and can do more good for the cause where the Lord has placed them, than anywhere else.'" Now note this particularly poignant message: "'God is using more than one people for the accomplishment of His great and marvelous work. The Latter-day Saints cannot do it all. It is too vast, too arduous for any one people.'" Elder Whitney then pointed out that we have no warfare with other churches. "'They are our partners in a certain sense.'"[27]

> "God is using more than one people for the accomplishment of His great and marvelous work. The Latter-day Saints cannot do it all. It is too vast, too arduous for any one people."
> —Elder Orson F. Whitney

5. It does not mean that God-fearing Christians who are not Latter-day Saints will have no claim on heaven. The Latter-day Saints do not in any way minimize or deny the reality of another person's experience with the Spirit of God, nor should we question the legitimacy of another's commitment to Jesus Christ. Christians who are somewhat acquainted with our beliefs might well respond at this point: "Yes, but

do you believe that persons of other faiths will inherit the celestial kingdom?" Latter-day Saints do believe that baptism by proper authority is necessary for entrance into the highest heaven; the baptismal ordinance is an outward expression of one's personal inward covenant with Christ and acceptance of his gospel.

At the same time, our doctrine affirms that each person will receive all of the light, knowledge, divine attributes, powers, and heavenly rewards they desire to receive, either in this life or the next. Those who seek with all their soul to come unto Christ will be welcomed eventually into his presence. One who earnestly yearns to qualify for the highest of glory hereafter will have that opportunity. That means that a man or woman who is true to the light they have here will open themselves to greater light in days to come. Indeed, ours is, without question, the most broad and expansive and optimistic perspective on who will be saved. By revelation, we know that other than those who defect to perdition, the Lord will save all the works of his hands (Doctrine and Covenants 76:40–43).

6. Our belief that we are "the only true and living church" does not mean that we as Latter-day Saints desire to face social, moral, and family challenges on our own. While on the one hand The Church of Jesus Christ of Latter-day Saints is charged to "stand independent above all other creatures beneath the celestial world" (Doctrine and Covenants 78:14), we strive earnestly to work together with men and women of other faiths to stand up and speak out against the rising tide of secularism, immorality, and ethical relativism that are spreading in our world. Together with most conservative Christian groups, we are persuaded that the changes to be made in our society can only come about "from the inside out"— through the transforming powers of Jesus Christ.[28] Indeed, I am persuaded that if we allow doctrinal differences, stereotyping, and demonizing of those who are different from ourselves to prevent us from joining hands in halting the erosion of time-honored moral and family values, Lucifer will win a major victory.

"ONLY TRUE CHURCH": WHAT IT DOES MEAN

What, then, *does* the revelation mean when it states that The Church of Jesus Christ of Latter-day Saints is "the only true and living church upon the face of the whole earth"?

1. "The word *only*," Elder Neal A. Maxwell wrote, "asserts a uniqueness and singularity" about the Church "as the exclusive ecclesiastical, authority-bearing agent for our Father in heaven in this dispensation."[29]

The word *true* is derived from the Old English word *treowe*, meaning "honest, upright, virtuous, straightforward, loyal, faithful, steady and steadfast, constant, fitting, proper, consistent with fact, conforming with reality, conforming to a standard or pattern, accurately positioned, germane, correctly balanced or aligned, precise, and secure." *True* is related closely to such words as *trust*, *truce*, and *betrothed*.[30] Thus to refer to the restored Church as "the only true church" is to speak of it as being the most steady, sure, and solid institution on earth, the closest to the pattern of the primitive Christian church in terms of dispensing the mind and will of God and enjoying his complete approbation.

> To refer to the restored Church as "the only true church" is to speak of it as being the most steady, sure, and solid institution on earth, the closest to the pattern of the primitive Christian church.

"When the Lord used the designation '*true*,'" Elder Maxwell pointed out, "he implied that the doctrines of the Church and its authority are not just partially true, but true as measured by divine standards. The Church is not, therefore, conceptually compromised by having been made up from doctrinal debris left over from another age, nor is it comprised of mere fragments of the true faith. It is based upon the *fulness* of the gospel of him whose *name* it bears, thus passing the two tests for proving his church that were given by Jesus during his visit to the Nephites (3 Nephi 27:8).

"When the word *living* is used," Elder Maxwell observed, "it carries a divinely deliberate connotation. The Church is neither dead nor dying. Nor is it even wounded. The Church, like the living God who established it, is alive, aware, and functioning. It is not a museum that houses a fossilized faith; rather, it is a kinetic kingdom characterized by living faith in living disciples."[31]

2. It means that doctrinal finality rests with apostles and prophets, not theologians or scholars. One professor of religion at a Christian institution remarked to me, "You know, Bob, one of the things I love about my way of life as a religious academician is that no one is looking over my shoulder to check my doctrine and analyze the truthfulness of my teachings. Because there is no organizational hierarchy to which I am required to answer, I am free to write and declare whatever I choose." I nodded kindly and chose not to respond at the time. I have thought since then, however, that what my friend perceives to be a marvelous academic freedom can become license to interpret a scriptural passage in a myriad of ways, resulting in interpretations as diverse as the backgrounds, training, and proclivities of the persons involved. This is doctrinal chaos. There are simply too many ambiguous sections of scripture to "let the Bible speak for itself." That was, in fact, young Joseph Smith's dilemma: "The teachers of religion of the different sects understood the same passages of scripture so differently as to destroy all confidence in settling [his religious questions] by an appeal to the Bible" (Joseph Smith–History 1:12).

In writing of *sola scriptura* (scripture alone) as a tenet of the Reformation, historian Randall Balmer observed that "Luther's sentiments created a demand for Scriptures in the vernacular, and Protestants ever since have insisted on interpreting the Bible for themselves, forgetting most of the time that they come to the text with their own set of cultural biases and personal agendas.

"Underlying this insistence on individual interpretation," Balmer continued, "is the assumption . . . that the plainest, most evident reading of the text is the proper one. Everyone becomes his or her own theologian. There is no longer any need to consult Augustine or Thomas Aquinas or Martin Luther about their understanding of various passages when you yourself are the final arbiter of what is the correct reading. This tendency, together with the absence of any authority structure within Protestantism, has created a kind of theological free-for-all, as various individuals or groups insist that *their* reading of the Bible is the only possible interpretation."[32]

• • •

As Latter-day Saints we face a particularly difficult challenge. We must be true to the word of the Lord to Joseph Smith and uphold our belief that ours is "the only true and living church upon the face of the whole earth, with which [the Lord is] well pleased, speaking unto the church collectively and not individually" (Doctrine and Covenants 1:30).[33] This principle really should not offend persons outside our own faith, at least not as much as it does. Doesn't the Roman Catholic Church believe itself to be the "only true church"? Do not those who hold to the Eastern Orthodox persuasion feel confident that they represent the purest version of the first-century Christian church? Do not our Jewish or Muslim brothers and sisters believe that their way of approaching God or Allah is the proper and correct path to take? Latter-day Saints accept the language of the Lord Jesus that none of the churches on earth in 1820 possessed the fulness of the gospel of Christ. By necessity we accept the burden of declaring this truth to persons we meet throughout the world. In fact, it is in our distinctiveness that we as a people can make a contribution to the larger religious conversation.

President Gordon B. Hinckley offered the following tender counsel: "The Lord said that this is the only true and living Church upon the face of the earth with which He is well pleased. I didn't say that. Those are His words. The Prophet Joseph was told that the other sects were wrong. Those are not my words. Those are the Lord's words. But *they are hard words for those of other faiths. We don't need to exploit them.* We just need to be kind and good and gracious people to others, showing by our example the great truth of that which we believe."[34]

Chapter 6

"ALL THEIR CREEDS"

The Lord Jesus Christ responded to fourteen-year-old Joseph Smith's simple question—simple, but with terribly profound implications. He was told in no uncertain terms that he must join none of the churches. One wonders whether the Lord's response might have shocked the young seeker. Join none of them? Surely there must be one church with which he could affiliate, perhaps at least mostly acceptable to the Lord. But the Savior commanded otherwise, and he did so in bold denunciation: "I was answered that I must join none of them, for they were all wrong; and the Personage who addressed me said that *all their creeds were an abomination in his sight; that those professors were all corrupt*" (Joseph Smith–History 1:19; emphasis added).[1]

WHAT IS A CREED?

The word *creed* is taken from the Latin word *credo,* which means "I believe." In short, a creed is a statement of belief. There is nothing evil about a creed, as long as what is taught is true. For example, Doctrine and Covenants 20:17–36 is a kind of creedal statement of doctrine to be found in the Book of Mormon and the revelations given to the Prophet Joseph Smith. When the early missionaries of this dispensation went into the world to declare the glad tidings of the Restoration, they frequently referred to these verses and taught from them.

In speaking of the fifth lecture in the *Lectures on Faith*, which deals with the Godhead, Elder Bruce R. McConkie stated: "Using the holy scriptures as the recorded source of the knowledge of God, knowing what the Lord has revealed to them of old in visions and by the power of the Spirit, and writing as guided by that same Spirit, *Joseph Smith and the early brethren of this dispensation prepared a creedal statement on the Godhead*. It is without question the most excellent summary of revealed and eternal truth relative to the Godhead that is now extant in mortal language. In it is set forth the mystery of Godliness; that is, it sets forth the personalities, missions, and ministries of those holy beings who comprise the supreme presidency of the universe."[2]

What do we suppose the Savior had in mind when he condemned their creeds as "an abomination in my sight"? Webster's 1828 *American Dictionary of the English Language* defined the word *abominable* as "very hateful, detestable, loathsome." Other synonyms are "odious" or "offensive." *Abomination* is also defined as "the object of detestation." Other definitions include "defilement, pollution in a physical sense, or evil doctrines and practices, which are moral defilements, idols and idolatry." It would be difficult for us to find a more pejorative word.

The creeds of the Christian church were those doctrinal formulations and theological pronouncements devised at church councils, intended to clarify what the correct interpretation of a given doctrine was, and thus, at the same time, to identify heresy and heretical interpretations. The earliest of these was the Apostles Creed, dating to about A.D. 140. Christian church councils, from which theological teachings derived, include the following:

- The Nicene Council (A.D. 325)
- The Councils of Constantinople (A.D. 381, 553, 681)
- The Athanasian Creed (A.D. late 400s to early 500s)
- The Councils of Carthage and Orange (A.D. 419 and 529)

- The Councils of Ephesus (A.D. 431, 449, 475)
- The Council of Chalcedon (A.D. 451)

There followed, during the Protestant Reformation, the Heidelberg Confession (1563), the Thirty-Nine Articles of Religion of the Church of England (1563), and, within a hundred years, the Presbyterian Church's Westminster Confession of Faith (1647).[3]

Perhaps the greatest harm was done when philosophers and theologians began to shroud the God of heaven by making a mystery of him. Once we tamper with the identity of Deity, we automatically open ourselves to misconceptions concerning the nature of mortal men and women, for we are the spirit children of Deity. The doctrinal dominos then begin to fall. Near the end of his prophetic ministry, Joseph Smith enunciated the following profound truths at the funeral for King Follett: "*There are but a very few beings in the world who understand rightly the character of God. The great majority of mankind do not comprehend anything, either that which is past, or that which is to come, as it respects their relationship to God. They do not know, neither do they understand the nature of that relationship. . . . If men do not comprehend the character of God, they do not comprehend themselves.*"[4]

Professor Rodney Turner, a late friend and Brigham Young University colleague, wrote some years ago: "To know what God is is to know what man is—and what he may become. The loss of this knowledge goes far to explain the present plight of humanity. *Man, like water, cannot rise higher than his beginnings.* If an ever-increasing number of men and women are choosing to wallow in the mire of carnality, we must not forget that they are taught that the human race was spawned in mire. *We have little desire to reach for the stars if we do not believe that we came from the stars.* That we did is the message of the Restored Gospel. This is why The Church of Jesus Christ of Latter-day Saints testifies that—where the valiant are concerned—*the origin of man is the destiny of man.*"[5]

THE PERILS AND PAINS OF CREEDALISM

A notable feature of Joseph Smith's age was a desire on the part of many Americans to jettison the theological formulations, the doctrinal creeds and confessions (statements of belief) of Christendom, to focus less on *orthodoxy* (correct theology) and more on *orthopraxy* (correct practice of religion in daily life). In 1756 John Adams, later second president of the United States, wrote: "Where do we find a precept in the Gospel requiring ecclesiastical synods, convocations, councils, decrees, creeds, confessions, oaths, subscriptions and whole cartloads of other trumpery, that we find religion encumbered with in these days?"[6] His wife, Abigail, wrote in 1818: "When will mankind be convinced that true religion is from the heart, between man and his Creator and not the imposition of man or creeds or tests?"[7] Thomas Jefferson in 1822 was even more harsh in his denunciation of creeds: "I have never permitted myself to meditate a specified creed," he stated. "These formulas have been the bane and ruin of the Christian church, its own fatal invention which, through so many ages, made of Christendom a slaughterhouse, and at this day divides it into castes of indistinguishable hatred to one another."[8]

> Religious creeds . . . tend to create distance between the children of God—to separate and divide people on the basis of belief; to draw strict lines in the sand between what is "orthodox" and what is "heresy"; to foster pride and antagonism on the part of those who wear their beliefs like a badge of belonging.

There is no question but that the Savior denounced religious creeds because of the doctrinal damage they have inflicted. As President Dallin H. Oaks has noted, they fostered confusion on matters of doctrine, particularly the nature of the Godhead, as well as men and women's relationship to Deity.[9] There is, however, another problem with creeds—they tend to create distance between the children of God—to separate and divide people on the basis of belief; to draw strict lines in the sand between what is "orthodox" and what is "heresy"; to foster pride and antagonism on the part of those who wear their beliefs like a badge of belonging.

Joseph Smith was very clear about his own feelings regarding religious creeds. Consider the following remarks from the Prophet:

"'Wherein do you differ from other sects?' Because we believe the Bible, and all other sects profess to believe their interpretations of the Bible, and their creeds."[10]

"[The] first and fundamental principle of our holy religion is, that we believe that we have a right to embrace all, and every item of truth, without limitation or without being circumscribed or prohibited by the creeds or superstitious notions of men, or by the dominations of one another, when that truth is clearly demonstrated to our minds."[11]

In speaking with Josiah Butterfield, Brother Joseph stated, "The most prominent difference in sentiment between the Latter-day Saints and sectarians was, that the latter were all circumscribed by some peculiar creed, which deprived its members the privilege of believing anything not contained therein, whereas the Latter-day Saints . . . are ready to believe all true principles that exist, as they are made manifest from time to time."[12]

"THOSE PROFESSORS WERE ALL CORRUPT"

The Savior declared to young Joseph that "those professors were all corrupt" (Joseph Smith–History 1:19). In speaking to students at Brigham Young University in 1985 about the Prophet Joseph's First Vision and the words of the Lord to him, Elder W. Grant Bangerter of the Seventy asked: "Do we believe that all ministers of other churches are corrupt? Of course not. Joseph Smith certainly did not intend that. By reading the passage carefully, we find that *the Lord Jesus Christ was referring to those ministers who were quarrelling and arguing about which church was true—that is, the particular group with which Joseph Smith was involved.*"

Elder Bangerter continued: "They were drawing (the Savior said it, not Joseph Smith) 'near to me with their lips, but their hearts are far from me, they teach for doctrines the commandments of men, having a form of godliness, but they deny the power thereof' ([Joseph Smith–History] 1:19)." However, he concluded, it is a fact that "Joseph Smith was roughly handled by the members and ministers of various prominent religions, who tarred and feathered him, took up arms against him and his people, imprisoned him, and finally instigated his murder and martyrdom. Some of them still follow a similar course of ridicule and active antagonism. This condition must not warp our own understanding and conduct."[13]

Now, let's look more carefully at the specific concerns the Lord spoke of.

"THEY DRAW NEAR TO ME WITH THEIR LIPS"

Such professors of Christianity may talk the talk but often do not walk the walk; what they preach is one thing, and how they live is another. In my own experience, I have come across people, both within and beyond our own Church, who profess with all their hearts that they are disciples of Christ, yet theirs is a judgmental, critical, accusing, and angry way of dealing with persons who may disagree with them or who read or interpret the Bible differently. In short, the way they treat people is anything but Christian.

> *I have come across people, both within and beyond our own Church, who profess with all their hearts that they are disciples of Christ, yet theirs is a judgmental, critical, accusing, and angry way of dealing with persons who may disagree with them or who read or interpret the Bible differently. In short, the way they treat people is anything but Christian.*

Anyone who attends a general conference of The Church of Jesus Christ of Latter-day Saints in Salt Lake City is able to witness the behavior of street preachers who attack and accuse and criticize members of the Church who are simply attempting to cross the street to the Conference Center. Almost all of these antagonists are "Christian" people who feel a sense of divine call to put us in our place; to point out where we are guilty of heresy; to denounce us as a dangerous cult; to basically trample upon anything we may hold dear. A few years back, my wife, Shauna, and I were making our way to the Conference Center when we encountered a man who was holding a copy of the Book of Mormon high above his head. He began to rip pages from the book, throwing them on the ground, stomping on them, and yelling, "This is what I think of your stupid Book of Mormon!"

At first I felt anger in my heart toward the man, but the anger was quickly replaced with sadness for any human being who would act in such a way while supposing he was rendering service to God. The Savior himself put it this way: "Out of the abundance of the heart the mouth speaketh" (Matthew 12:34). Without question, the best way to assess to what extent we are Christians is to observe how we speak of and to others and in general how we treat our brothers and sisters.

Elder Carlos E. Asay suggested that "perhaps some of the professors were 'humble followers of Christ; nevertheless they [were] led, that in many instances they [did] err because they [were] taught by the precepts of men' (2 Nephi 28:14). Perhaps honest efforts were being made, but whatever was being done was insufficient 'to teach any man the right way' (2 Nephi 25:28)."[14]

THE COMMANDMENTS OF MEN

The Lord's words were, "They teach for doctrines the commandments of men, having a form of godliness, but they deny the power thereof" (Joseph Smith–History 1:19). In my mind, this pronouncement is linked to the Savior's remarks about the creeds of Christianity. When the language of a creed becomes sacred—in the sense that biblical doctrine is determined, evaluated, and interpreted by the words of the creed—then the creed becomes more significant than the words of the Bible and people have begun to teach for doctrine the commandments of men.

Think about a person who is earnestly seeking to better understand the character and nature of the Almighty. Now suppose that she leans and relies heavily upon creedal formulations in her scriptural interpretation of Deity. In doing so, she has allowed the creed to trump the scripture. Consider what happens when the following creedal notions are superimposed over scriptural teachings about God:

> When the language of a creed becomes sacred—in the sense that biblical doctrine is determined, evaluated, and interpreted by the words of the creed—then the creed becomes more significant than the words of the Bible and people have begun to teach for doctrine the commandments of men.

He is without body, parts, and passions.
He is immutable (unchanging over time, is unable to change).
He is impassible (cannot suffer or feel pain).
He is ineffable (too great to be explained or expressed in words).
He is incomprehensible and unknowable.

By definition, such a God will remain forever unknown. Once again, we recall the words of Jesus in his great high priestly prayer: "And this is life eternal, that they might know thee the only true God, and Jesus Christ whom thou hast sent" (John 17:3).

DENYING THE POWER

"They have a form of godliness, but they deny the power thereof" (Joseph Smith–History 1:19). To *deny* is to contradict or contravene; to say that something is not true, not what it seems or purports to be. Or it is to stand in opposition to something. From one perspective, to deny the power of God is to say or act as though it does not exist or is not necessary. To deny the power of God is to contend that no priesthood or divine authority is necessary in order to officiate in the Lord's kingdom. To deny the power of God is to attempt to silence him, to resist any and all additional divine communication. The Prophet Joseph remarked, "I want to come up into the presence of God, and learn all things; but *the creeds set up stakes, and say, 'Hitherto shalt thou come, and no further'*; which I cannot subscribe to."[15] Nephi warned of a time when people would cry out, "All is well in Zion" and "We have received the word of God, and we need no more of the word of God, for we have enough!" (2 Nephi 28:21, 29).

> To deny the power of God is to contend that no priesthood or divine authority is necessary in order to officiate in the Lord's kingdom.

• • •

The restoration of divine truth concerning God our Father is not at all about lowering a high and holy God to the level of lowly and languishing humanity; it is about worshipping a Being with whom we can identify, one who may be known, understood, and approached, one who, like his Beloved Son, can be "touched with the feeling of our infirmities" (Hebrews 4:15). If it is, as Jesus said, life eternal to know God and to know Jesus Christ (see John 17:3), how disappointing to find that the wonders and ways of the Godhead have been shrouded in mystery, never to be understood.

President Gordon B. Hinckley, one of Joseph Smith's prophetic successors, rejoiced: "To me it is a significant and marvelous thing that in establishing and opening this dispensation our Father did so with a revelation of himself and of his Son Jesus Christ, as if to say to all the world that he was weary of the attempts of men, earnest though these attempts might have been, to define and describe him. . . . The experience of Joseph Smith in a few moments in the grove on a spring day in 1820, brought more light and knowledge and understanding of the personality and reality and substance of God and his Beloved Son than men had arrived at during centuries of speculation."[16]

The Restoration took place largely so that "every man [and woman] might speak in the name of God the Lord, even the Savior of the world; that faith also might increase in the earth" (Doctrine and Covenants 1:20–21). The doors to heavenly light and religious understanding—especially and including our true relationship to Deity—began to be opened wide in a grove in upstate New York in 1820, and once again men and women, boys and girls were welcomed into the light of revealed truth.

> *The doors to heavenly light and religious understanding—especially and including our true relationship to Deity—began to be opened wide in a grove in upstate New York in 1820, and once again men and women, boys and girls were welcomed into the light of revealed truth.*

Chapter 7

AFTER THE VISION

We can imagine that after the First Vision the youthful prophet would never have viewed the world in the same way. His previous existence of eating, sleeping, clearing the land, constructing homes and farm buildings, plowing fields, scrimping and saving every spare penny so that the family could stay alive—those things would not have been altered in any appreciable way: the Smiths still needed to expend every ounce of energy to stay afloat. The magnificent theophany that he had experienced, however, would of necessity create a new worldview for Joseph, would bring to pass what we might call a massive paradigm shift. He would now look upon the things of this world with what might be called anointed eyes. Nothing would ever be quite the same.

JOSEPH IS WEAKENED BY THE EXPERIENCE

In his official history (1838), the Prophet Joseph indicated that following the vision, after the Father and the Son had ascended, "When I came to myself again, I found myself lying on my back, looking up into heaven. When the light had departed, I had no strength" (Joseph Smith–History 1:20). David Nye White (1843) stated that the Prophet had explained to him that "when I came to myself, I was sprawling on my back, and it was some time before my strength returned." Alexander

Neibaur's brief account (1844) said that Joseph "endeavored to arise but felt uncommonly feeble."[1] Joseph went on to say that "when the light had departed, I had no strength; but soon recovering in some degree, I went home" (Joseph Smith–History 1:20).

On one occasion, the Prophet Joseph spoke of how he had been weakened and actually turned pale after he had blessed a group of children. He likened it to the experience of Jesus recorded in Luke 8 of healing the woman who had had "an issue of blood" for twelve years. The woman's faith was so strong she was convinced that if she could but touch the hem of his garment, she would be healed. When she touched his garment, Jesus stopped in his tracks, turned about, and asked, "Who touched me?" The apostles quickly reminded the Lord that a large crowd of people were surrounding him. He responded, "Virtue is gone out of me." Joseph explained, "*The virtue referred to here is the spirit of life; and a man that exercises great faith in administering to the sick, blessing little children, or confirming, is liable to become weakened.*"[2]

The First Vision experience of the boy Joseph meant he had just been involved in an event of such spiritual magnitude that it was necessary for him to be *transfigured* in order to abide the glory and power of the first two members of the Godhead. It was necessary for God to fill him with an additional spiritual strength and power, as He did with Moses on the mountain (Moses 1:8–10). The same was true with Nephi, son of Lehi. To his ever-complaining brothers, who had ridiculed him regarding his ability to build a ship, Nephi stated, "Behold, *I am full of the Spirit of God, insomuch that my frame has no strength*" (1 Nephi 17:47; emphasis added).

In speaking of Joseph Smith's experience, Truman G. Madsen pointed out that "Joseph was filled with a Spirit which enabled him to endure the presence of God. Is that Spirit enervating or is it energizing? My considered answer is 'Yes.' It is both. It demands from us a concentration and a surrender comparable to nothing else possible in this life. But it also confers great capacities that transcend our finite mental, spiritual, and physical powers."³ Brother Madsen gave as an illustration of this phenomenon what happened to Sidney Rigdon after he and Joseph had seen the vision of the glories. Philo Dibble was present to witness the glory and listen to the reports of the Prophet and Sidney as they recounted various elements of the vision. "Joseph sat firmly and calmly all the time in the midst of a magnificent glory," Brother Dibble reported, "but Sidney sat limp and pale, apparently as limber as a rag, observing which, Joseph remarked, smilingly, 'Sidney is not used to it as I am.'"⁴

"PRESBYTERIANISM IS NOT TRUE"

Upon returning to his home, young Joseph "leaned up to the fireplace," and his mother inquired what the matter was. Joseph said, "'Never mind, all is well—I am well enough off.' [He] then said to [his] mother, 'I have learned for myself that Presbyterianism is not true'" (Joseph Smith–History 1:20). What, exactly, would have been incorrect within Presbyterianism? A brief paragraph from the 1647 Westminster Confession of Faith, the theological creed subscribed to by the Presbyterian Church, follows:

"There is but one only living and true God, who is infinite in being and perfection, *a most pure spirit, invisible,* without body, parts, or passions, immutable [unalterable, changeless], immense, eternal, *incomprehensible,* almighty, most wise, most holy, most free, most absolute, working all things according to the counsel of his own immutable and most righteous will, for his own glory; most loving, gracious, merciful, long-suffering, abundant in goodness and truth, forgiving iniquity, transgression, and sin; the rewarder of them that diligently seek him; and withal most just and terrible in his judgments; hating all sin, and who will by no means clear the guilty."⁵

Oh, how interesting it would have been to listen in on that conversation with Lucy Mack Smith. Surely much more was said between mother and son. As we mentioned earlier, Lucy and three of the Smith children had joined the Presbyterian Church, and so a comment like Joseph's would have certainly prompted Mother Smith to ask, at least, "What do you mean? Why would you say that? How do you know?" Although Joseph does not mention any additional discussion, it might have been the case that he described, as best he could, what he had just experienced in the Sacred Grove, including what he had learned about all of the churches. In her history of her son, Mother Smith includes only what we have in Joseph's 1838 account and says nothing more about Presbyterianism in that account.[6]

FILLED WITH JOY AND LOVE

In his 1835 account Joseph mentioned that "a pillar of fire appeared above my head. It presently rested down upon me and *filled me with joy unspeakable.*" In his earliest account (1832) Joseph recorded that after the appearance, "*my soul was filled with love, and for many days I could rejoice with great joy, and the Lord was with me.*"[7] It is not uncommon for a person to be filled with joy and the love of God following a profound spiritual experience. I am reminded of the occasion when young Lorenzo Snow underwent a powerful and dramatic spiritual rebirth. He had been baptized and confirmed a member of The Church of Jesus Christ of Latter-day Saints, but he had not obtained the depth of witness and conviction he had expected would be given him. He indicated that on a particular occasion he was feeling disappointed and even tempted not to have his evening prayer but finally chose to pray anyway. "I had no sooner opened my lips in an effort to pray, than I heard a sound, just above my head, like the rustling of silken robes, and immediately the Spirit of God descended upon me, from the crown of my head to the soles of my feet, and *O, the joy and happiness I felt!*"[8]

After his vision, Joseph felt an overflowing love and a sweet, comforting peace. To teach that "God is love" (1 John 4:8), as did

John the Beloved, is to say that our Heavenly Father and his Son, Jesus Christ, are, as exalted and perfected individuals, the very embodiment of love. Jesus taught at the Last Supper that he is the way, the truth, and the life (John 14:6). It isn't just that Jesus will teach us the way; *he is the way*. It isn't just that Jesus teaches the truth; *he is the truth*. It isn't just that Jesus extends life to us; *he is the life*. And it isn't simply that our Father in Heaven and his Only Begotten Son extend love to us; *they are love*, the very embodiment of love, perfect and pure and everlasting love, which we call charity (Moroni 7:47; compare Ether 12:32–34). One cannot be in the presence of a holy, exalted Being and not be filled to overflowing with the love he feels toward his children. And so it was with young Joseph Smith.

> One cannot be in the presence of a holy, exalted Being and not be filled to overflowing with the love he feels toward his children. And so it was with young Joseph Smith.

"MANY OTHER THINGS"

Another comment by the Prophet Joseph that, though brief, speaks volumes: "He again forbade me to join with any of them." Now note what follows: "And many other things did he say unto me, which I cannot write at this time" (Joseph Smith–History 1:20). We do not know how long Joseph Smith was caught up in vision with God the Father and Jesus Christ the Son. Was it moments? Hours?

However long the duration of the transcendent experience was, we can rest assured that enough was said and heard to prepare young Joseph Smith for the monumental task that lay before him. From the Wentworth letter (1842) we read, "I was expressly commanded to 'go not after [the churches],' at the same time receiving a promise that the fulness of the gospel should at some future time be made known unto me."[9]

Further, we know that God "revealed as much as Joseph was

capacitated to receive. The Lord dealt with this young man as parents do when they wish to instruct their children on any subject. You do not pour out volumes of instruction on them all at once, but impart to them according to their capacity." The Lord "imparted enough to let him know that the whole Christian world was without authority."[10]

PERSECUTION FOLLOWS

Joseph indicated in 1832 that after the vision "the Lord was with me, but [I] could find none that would believe the heavenly vision."[11] Orson Pratt stated that Joseph "began to relate it to some of his nearest friends, and he was told by some of the ministers who came to him to enquire about it, that there was no such thing as the visitation of heavenly messengers, that God gave no new revelation, and that no visions could be given to the children of men in this age." Now note Elder Orson Pratt's words: "*This was like telling him that there was no such thing as seeing, or feeling, or hearing, or tasting, or smelling. Why? Because he knew positively to the contrary.*"[12]

> "Now, the devil did not particularly care how many good principles people retained, so long as they should deny one of the most important principles of heaven. Cut off communication from the Lord, shut up the heavens, keep angels out of the question concerning any more new communication to be given to the children of men, and the devil has accomplished his object."
> —Elder Orson Pratt

Mary Isabella Hales Horne spoke of an occasion when she heard the Prophet describe "his first vision when the Father and the Son appeared to him. . . . While he was relating the circumstances the Prophet's countenance lightened up, and so wonderful a power accompanied his words that everyone who heard them felt his influence and power."[13]

Elder Orson Pratt spoke at another time about a position that had been taken by the Reformers—biblical sufficiency—but "that there was to be no more revelation from heaven; that the canon of Scripture was full. . . . Now, the devil did not particularly care how many good principles people retained, so long as they should deny one of the most important principles of heaven. Cut off communication from the Lord, shut up the heavens, keep angels out of the question concerning any more new communication to be given to the children of men, and the devil has accomplished his object."[14]

Joseph recorded that on one occasion he "happened to be in company with one of the Methodist preachers, who was very active in the before mentioned religious excitement. . . . I took occasion to give him an account of the vision which I had had. I was greatly surprised at his behavior; he treated my communication not only lightly, but with great contempt, saying it was all of the devil, that there were no such things as visions or revelations in these days; that all such things had ceased with the apostles, and that there would never be any more of them" (Joseph Smith–History 1:21).

We can appreciate why a Protestant minister would have treated Joseph's report of his vision "lightly." As we pointed out earlier, the Smiths were immersed in a visionary culture, in which people often "claimed to have heavenly visions from time to time."[15] In other words, what we may think of now as Joseph's unusual claim was not so very unusual, and the minister supposed that Joseph's report of a vision was as unfounded and imagined as many others during those years. But of the devil? What a tragedy that a man of the cloth would so quickly assume that a boy's claim of a heavenly manifestation is automatically to be considered diabolical. Nephi, son of Lehi, had warned of just such a day: "They shall contend one with another; and their priests shall contend one with another, and they shall teach with their learning, and deny the Holy Ghost, which giveth utterance" (2 Nephi 28:4).

This attitude derives from a theological position known as *cessationism*. Related to the word *cease*, *cessationism* means "to pause or stop," in this case, the pausing or stopping of spiritual gifts and spiritual manifestations, a position taken by many in the Christian world even today. According to Alexander Neibaur's account, young Joseph "told the Methodist" about his encounter with the Father and the Son, and that the minister "said this was not an age for God to reveal himself in vision. Revelation has ceased with the New Testament." Or, as David Nye White recorded, "when [Joseph] went home and told the people that I had a revelation, and that all the churches were corrupt, they persecuted me, and they have persecuted me ever since. They thought to put me down, but they haven't succeeded, and they can't do it."¹⁶

> Why do those who attack us with their anti-Mormon tracts, video presentations, and seminars hate us so much?
>
> Well, to be honest with you, we started the fight. Joseph Smith's announcement of what he had learned in the Sacred Grove drove the initial wedge between us and the rest of Christendom.

We can understand why those who earnestly contended that revelation and gifts had ceased would dismiss and disagree wholeheartedly with the boy Joseph. But disagree *violently*, so as to inflict bodily harm to the person claiming such manifestations? There must have been something deeper, something beneath the surface, at stake here. And so there was and is. Elder Orson Pratt stated: "Why should they feel such concern and anxiety in relation to his testimony as to persecute him, a boy not quite fifteen years of age? The reason was obvious—*if that testimony* [of Joseph] *was true, not one of their churches was the true church of Christ*. No wonder, then, that they began to persecute, point the finger of scorn, and say—'There goes the visionary boy.'"¹⁷

It is not uncommon for me to be asked, "Why do those who attack us with their anti-Mormon tracts, video presentations, and seminars hate us so much?" Why do they spend millions of dollars in an endeavor that has clearly become a cottage industry? When asked that question in recent years and without intending any offense, I have replied, "Well, to be honest with you, we started the fight. Joseph Smith's announcement of what he had learned in the Sacred Grove drove the initial wedge between us and the rest of Christendom." American religious historian R. Laurence Moore wrote, "If sustained controversy denotes cultural importance, then Mormons were as significant as any other religious group in nineteenth-century America."[18]

Historian Jan Shipps, a Methodist, has written much on the restored Church. She commented that "unlike the restorationist understandings of the Campbellite, Seventh-day Baptist, and other primitivist movements, . . . Mormonism's understanding of itself as *the* (not 'a') restoration proceeded from the assumption that restoration could and would come about when *and only when* direct communication between humanity and divinity was reopened. This is to say that before restoration could occur, one who could speak for God, a prophet, would have to come forth."[19]

A beloved friend of mine, Professor Richard J. Mouw of Fuller Theological Seminary, pointed out most perceptively that a person cannot understand the followers of Joseph Smith and what makes us tick by simply discussing, for example, our new books of scripture. There is more. "For Mormonism, this reliance on writings—sacred 'pages'—is secondary. What they see as primary is *the office of the prophet*. The most important thing to Mormons about their early history isn't that Joseph Smith dug up the golden plates containing the Book of Mormon in the early decades of the nineteenth century. More importantly, Mormonism teaches that *in the person of Joseph Smith the ancient office of prophet was restored*."[20]

HESITATION TO SPEAK OF THE VISION

Joseph explained, "I soon found . . . that my telling the story had excited a great deal of prejudice against me among professors of religion, and was the cause of great persecution, which continued to increase" (Joseph Smith–History 1:22). That the expression "professors of religion" refers to church leaders in Joseph's vicinity and not to university professors of theology is made clear when we read later in his history: "We had been threatened with being *mobbed*, from time to time, and this, too, *by professors of religion*" (Joseph Smith–History 1:75; emphasis added).

Clearly as time went by, the young prophet became extremely hesitant to mention the First Vision in large public gatherings. For the most part, he was very cautious about sharing with everyone matters that would not be well received, matters that most persons were not prepared to receive. In a later revelation, Joseph was counseled by the Lord, "Unto you it is given to know the mysteries of the kingdom, but unto the world it is not given to know them" (Doctrine and Covenants 42:65; compare JST, Matthew 7:9–11).

In 1980 a significant article by James B. Allen of the Brigham Young University history department appeared in the *Journal of Mormon History*.[21] "It is worth noting," Professor Allen stated, "that Joseph Smith himself never used the First Vision to illustrate his own expanded teachings about God," namely, that God was a glorified Being of flesh and bone. Allen pointed out that even Elder Parley P. Pratt, in his 1855 masterwork, *Key to the Science of Theology*, "completely ignored the vision in its extensive treatment of the Godhead."[22] In addition, when Elder Franklin D. Richards and Brother James A. Little published their *Compendium of the Faith and Doctrines of The Church of Jesus Christ of Latter-day Saints* (1857)—a kind of precursor to Elder Bruce R. McConkie's *Mormon Doctrine* (1958)—they did not use the First Vision to illustrate the corporeal nature of God the Father.

Professor Allen suggested that George Q. Cannon, who served more than once as a counselor in the First Presidency, "was a sort of transition figure between first- and second-generation Mormon writers, and as early as 1880, he suggested that the vision could be used to teach children about the nature of their Creator."[23]

THE CANON IS EXPANDED

Within six years after the deaths of the Prophet Joseph and his brother Hyrum in 1844, the population of the Church had grown in an impressive manner. This was especially true in Great Britain. By 1850 Latter-day Saints who had settled in the Utah Territory numbered 11,380, with 6,157 of those in Salt Lake County. The number of Saints in Great Britain numbered 30,747. In fact, the number of Church members in the British Mission was almost four times as great in 1842 as it was in 1840, a result of the highly successful missionary efforts of members of the Quorum of the Twelve Apostles.[24]

One of the challenges that the Church in Great Britain faced at that time was the lack of Church literature among the members. A very small proportion of the people had their own scriptures. When Elder Franklin D. Richards of the Quorum of the Twelve Apostles replaced fellow apostle Orson Pratt as president of the British Mission and traveled among the Saints, it pained him to see how spiritually needy the people were. Brother Richards had his own set of scriptures, of course, as well as copies of many of the revelations and translations of the Prophet Joseph Smith. In 1851 President Richards compiled some of his favorite Restoration materials and had them published as a mission (not missionary) pamphlet that he called *The Pearl of Great Price*.

This collection consisted of extracts from the prophecy of Enoch (Moses 6:43–7:69); the words of God to Moses on an unnamed mountain (Moses 1); the book of Abraham, incorporating the Prophet's translation of Egyptian papyri, including Facsimiles 1, 2, and 3; the Prophet's inspired translation of Matthew 24 (today designated as Joseph Smith–Matthew); what we now know as Doctrine and Covenants 77, a series of questions and divine answers regarding the book of Revelation; extracts from the Prophet's 1838 history, what we know as Joseph Smith–History; portions of several revelations received by Joseph Smith, including those found today in Doctrine and Covenants 7, 20, 27, and 107; the Articles of Faith, found at the end of the Wentworth letter; and a poem written by John Jaques, a British convert, entitled "Truth," which we know today as the lyrics of the hymn "Oh Say, What Is Truth?"[25]

The Saints in Britain were thrilled with this marvelous potpourri of prophetic teachings. As many of these same Saints gathered to the Salt Lake Valley, they took with them their copies of *The Pearl of Great Price*. An interest, even fascination with this short but profound pamphlet grew among all the members of the Church. Under assignment from the First Presidency, in 1878 Elder Orson Pratt prepared the first American edition of the *Pearl of Great Price*. At the October 1880 general conference President George Q. Cannon, counselor to President John Taylor, proposed to the assembled members of the Church that the *Pearl of Great Price* be added to the the Latter-day Saint scriptural canon. Interestingly, in 1890 the thirteen Articles of Faith were presented separately to the Saints as a part of the standard works of the Church by Elder Franklin D. Richards. It appears there had been some confusion among Church members about the status of those thirteen statements of belief and practice.

> Like all canonized scripture (our standard works), Joseph Smith–History is binding upon the Saints in the sense that we are expected to believe it, teach it, and measure all other efforts at historical explanation of the early days of the Restoration by it.

Today the account of Joseph Smith's First Vision is a part of the canonized Pearl of Great Price, and thus the Saints accept as authoritative what we know as Joseph Smith–History. The word *canon* is taken from a Hebrew word meaning a measuring device or a rule, a ruler, or in this case, a rule of faith and practice. Like all canonized scripture (our standard works), Joseph Smith–History is binding upon the Saints in the sense that we are expected to believe it, teach it, and measure all other efforts at historical explanation of the early days of the Restoration by it.

In writing of the great importance of two visions having been added to our standard works in April 1976—Joseph Smith's vision of the celestial kingdom (Doctrine and Covenants 137) and Joseph F. Smith's vision of the redemption of the dead (Doctrine and Covenants 138), Elder Bruce R. McConkie explained that "all inspired sayings and writings are true and are and should be accepted and believed by all who call themselves Saints. But the revelations, visions, prophecies, and narrations selected and published for official use are thereby made binding upon the people in a particular sense. They become part of the standard works of the Church. They become the standards, the measuring rods, by which doctrine and procedure are determined."[26] And what is true of sections 137 and 138 of the Doctrine and Covenants is equally true of Joseph Smith–History, which contains the official account of the First Vision. It is holy scripture.

• • •

There is a loneliness associated with having been brought into spiritual experience and yet being constrained and even restrained from making all things known to those you know and love, a loneliness that some persons may never understand. There was so much that Joseph Smith, the Prophet of the Restoration, wanted to make known to the Saints. "It is my meditation all the day, and more than my meat and drink," he stated, "to know how I shall make the Saints of God comprehend the visions that roll like an overflowing surge before my mind. Oh! how I would delight to bring before you things which you never thought of!"[27]

It is hard even to imagine what the world would have been like had there been no Joseph Smith and thus no First Vision. "We honor Joseph Smith as the great Prophet of the Restoration," President Russell M. Nelson explained. "What was it that made him so great? He was foreordained from the foundation of the earth to reveal Jesus Christ to this generation! In previous generations, that responsibility was entrusted to men such as Adam, Noah, Enoch, Abraham, and Melchizedek. Each dispensation was known by the prophet who was chosen to reveal Jesus Christ to them. Note this important principle: *the Lord Jesus Christ and His prophets go together*. Or, to phrase that still another way, *if one were to separate the Lord from Joseph Smith, one would separate Joseph Smith from the source of his greatness*."[28]

Chapter 8

WHAT JOSEPH LEARNED

President George Q. Cannon described beautifully what young Joseph Smith Jr. experienced in the grove near his home: "The boy's faith in the promises of God had now deepened into knowledge. He had been assailed by the power of evil, until it seemed he must succumb—that the limit of human endurance was passed. And in that instant of deepest despair, he had been suddenly transported into the blaze of celestial light. He had seen with his own eyes the Father and the Son, with his own ears he had heard their eternal voices. Over this untaught youth at least, the heavens were no longer as brass. He had emerged from the maze of doubt and uncertainty in which he had so long groped, and had received positive assurances on the matter nearest his heart from Him, whom to know was anciently declared to be life eternal."[1]

LESSONS LEARNED FROM THE FIRST VISION

Let us draw some conclusions about doctrine, precepts, and principles that we learn as a result of the theophany in Palmyra:

1. A universal apostasy or falling away from the primitive gospel and teachings of Jesus Christ had taken place sometime after the deaths of the Savior and his apostles. This falling away had been prophesied by ancient prophets (see, for example, Amos 8:11–12; Isaiah 24:5).

In his earliest (1832) account, Joseph explained that "from the age of twelve years to fifteen I pondered many things in my heart concerning the situation of the world of mankind—the contentions and divisions, the wickedness and abominations and the darkness which pervaded the minds of mankind. . . . [B]y searching the scriptures, I found that mankind did not come unto the Lord, but that they had apostatized from the true and living faith, and there was no society or denomination that built upon the gospel of Jesus Christ, as recorded in the New Testament."² And of course we have in the official account (1838) mention of the churches all being wrong; that their creeds were offensive to God; that the hearts of the professors (local ministers) were far from the Lord; that some of what they teach is man-made and not heaven-sent; and, that while they have a form of godliness, "they deny the power thereof" (Joseph Smith–History 1:19; compare Doctrine and Covenants 1:15–17).

> A universal apostasy or falling away from the primitive gospel and teachings of Jesus Christ had taken place sometime after the deaths of the Savior and his apostles.

2. "There are no winners in wars of words," as Elder Carlos E. Asay of the Seventy pointed out years ago. "Joseph learned that there are no winners in the tumult of opinions regarding religious matters. Such contention plays into the hands of Satan because he is the 'father of contention' (3 Ne. 11:29). He is the devil who turns priest against priest and convert against convert, creating strife or engendering good feelings more pretended than real ([Joseph Smith–History] 1:6, 12). Moreover, Joseph verified the fact that critical issues pertaining to the Spirit cannot be settled alone by 'an appeal to the Bible' as long as teachers of the Bible understand 'the same passages of scripture so differently' ([Joseph Smith–History] 1:12)."³

3. The promise in James 1:5–6 was true: those who lack wisdom may ask of God and receive that wisdom, and our Heavenly Father will

never be impatient with anyone for asking. I believe there are certain prayers that our Eternal Father rushes to answer, those that are like music to his ears. For example, if I ask God to bless and strengthen me to become a more loving, more giving, more available husband, father, and grandfather, I believe he will in time bring about the changes in my heart I need to be more Christlike in those most important of relationships. If I ask to sense and recognize those who are prepared to receive the restored gospel—that is, if I ask faithfully for more frequent missionary opportunities—the opportunities will unfold. Why? Because this is the work of the Lord, and he wants all of his children to receive, at the appropriate time, every blessing that can come through the everlasting gospel. I believe if I, like Solomon, ask for wisdom (1 Kings 3:3–12), God will, over time, strengthen my conscience, educate my desires, shape my priorities, and form my judgment. He will bless me with wisdom.

Professor Joseph Fielding McConkie explained that young Joseph Smith's powerful reception of James 1:5 was "the Spirit of revelation directing Joseph Smith to inquire of the Lord; that is, a revelation directing him to receive a revelation. The experience could leave us wondering how often revelations have gone unclaimed because of our failure to heed the prompting to ask."[4]

President Russell M. Nelson posed a simple but deeply significant question to the Latter-day Saints. "Brothers and sisters," he began, "how can we become the men and women—the Christlike servants—the Lord needs us to be? How can we find answers to questions that perplex us? If Joseph Smith's transcendent experience in the Sacred Grove teaches us anything, it is that the heavens are open and that God speaks to His children.

> "If Joseph Smith's transcendent experience in the Sacred Grove teaches us anything, it is that the heavens are open and that God speaks to His children."
> —President Russell M. Nelson

"The Prophet Joseph Smith set a pattern for us to follow in resolving our questions. Drawn to the promise of James that if we lack wisdom we may ask of God, the boy Joseph took his question directly to Heavenly Father. *He sought personal revelation, and his seeking opened this last dispensation.*

"In like manner, what will your seeking open for you? What wisdom do you lack? What do you feel an urgent need to know or understand? Follow the example of the Prophet Joseph. Find a quiet place where you can regularly go. Humble yourself before God. Pour out your heart to your Heavenly Father. Turn to Him for answers and for comfort."[5]

4. The value of pondering holy scripture. There is no more moving and instructive statement of the power of pondering or meditation than that contained in the Prophet's words: "Never did any passage of scripture come with more power to the heart of man than this did at this time to mine. It seemed to enter with great force into every feeling of my heart. I reflected on it again and again, knowing that if any person needed wisdom from God, I did; for how to act I did not know, and unless I could get more wisdom than I then had, I would never know" (Joseph Smith–History 1:12). We must attend to what Joseph did: he read the scriptures, he took the statement of James and "likened" it to himself, and he reflected on it again and again. What a simple formula for gaining greater insight into the word of God, for receiving divine guidance.

It was while Nephi, son of Lehi, pondered upon what Lehi had received in his dream-vision that a panoramic vision burst upon Nephi. "For it came to pass after I had desired to know the things that my father had seen, and believing that the Lord was able to make them known unto me, as I sat pondering in mine heart I was caught away in the Spirit of the Lord, yea, into an exceedingly high mountain, which I never had before seen, and upon which I never had before set my foot" (1 Nephi 11:1).

What followed was a vision of the tree of life; of the virgin Mary and her Son, who would be the Redeemer of the world; the condescension of God; the mortal ministry of Jesus and his apostles; the rejection of the Savior by the Jews and his crucifixion; the great and spacious building; Christ's ministry among the Nephites; the destruction of the Nephite people; the formation and wicked acts of a great and abominable church; the great and abominable church's keeping back and taking away plain and precious truths from the Bible; the inspiration attending Christopher Columbus; the deliverance of the Gentile colonists in America from their mother Gentiles; and the future day when the Church of the Lamb would be found in all nations of the world. All because Nephi desired, believed, and pondered.

Another illustration of the power of pondering scripture is the experience that President Joseph F. Smith had while pondering upon the postmortal ministry of Jesus to the world of spirits, as described in 1 Peter 3:18–20 and 4:6. There was opened to President Smith one of the greatest and most informative doctrinal visions ever given, what we know as the vision of the redemption of the dead (Doctrine and Covenants 138).

5. Satan is neither myth nor metaphor but an actual being who is bent upon thwarting the plan of the Father. He will do all that he can to distract, deceive, discourage, and destroy the children of God. Joseph learned firsthand that the evil one is an "actual being from the unseen world" (Joseph Smith–History 1:16) who has great power. He stalks God's people and, with his evil minions, strives continuously to lead us away from the covenant path. The apostle Peter's counsel to us is wise: "Be sober, be vigilant; because your adversary the devil, as a roaring lion, walketh about, seeking whom he may devour" (1 Peter 5:8).

6. God has greater power than Satan, and all the forces of evil cannot block the advancement of the kingdom of God. Elder Orson Pratt's account of the First Vision says that "at first, he [Joseph] was severely tempted by the powers of darkness, which endeavored to overcome

him; but he continued to seek for deliverance, until darkness gave way from his mind; and he was enabled to pray, in fervency of the spirit, and in faith. And, while thus pouring out his soul, anxiously desiring an answer from God, he at length saw a very bright and glorious light in the heavens above."[6] No matter the intensity of the temptation or evil opposition, with God's help we can prevail.

In his 1842 account of the First Vision, Elder Orson Hyde expressed beautifully the young boy's deliverance from Satan's grasp: "The adversary then made several strenuous efforts to cool his ardent soul. He filled his mind with doubts and brought to mind all manner of inappropriate images to prevent him from obtaining the object of his endeavors; but *the overflowing mercy of God came to buoy him up and gave new impetus to his failing strength.*" Then, "the dark cloud soon parted and light and peace filled his frightened heart."[7]

7. The reality of the immortality of the soul. Before young Joseph stood Jesus Christ, the Only Begotten Son of God, in company with his Eternal Father. The testimony of the New Testament writers was that Jesus did in very deed rise from Joseph of Arimathea's tomb. That is, his eternal spirit was reunited with his now glorified and exalted body to stand evermore as the testimony that life continues after death; the Resurrection is an actual, real, and inseparable union of the body and the spirit; and this union results in the fulness of joy (see Doctrine and Covenants 93:33). Joseph could later add his conviction to that of the prophets who had preceded him: "And now, after the many testimonies which have been given of him, this is the testimony, last of all, which we give of him: That he lives!" (Doctrine and Covenants 76:22).

8. Salvation is in Christ. In the atrium of the Joseph Smith Building on the Brigham Young University campus is a beautiful statue of the young Joseph Smith kneeling in the grove. I was serving as dean of Religious Education at the time it was placed there (1997), and I recall clearly the extensive effort that was expended by the grounds crew at BYU to plant trees and shrubs in such a way that each time students

or visitors passed that quiet and beautiful spot they would be prompted to reflect on the theophany in Palmyra. I was asked to conduct the brief dedication ceremony and make a few comments. President Henry B. Eyring, then the Commissioner of Church Education and a member of the Quorum of the Twelve Apostles, spoke to those gathered and then offered a dedicatory prayer. "From studying the various accounts of the First Vision," he said, "we learn that young Joseph went into the grove not only to learn which church he should join but also to obtain forgiveness for his sins, *something he seems not to have understood how to do*. And in more than one account the Lord addressed the young truth seeker and said, 'Joseph, my son, thy sins are forgiven thee.'

"I hope that as young people through the generations see this statue," President Eyring continued, "they will realize . . . [that] this piece of art represents *that moment when Joseph Smith learned there was a way for the power of the Atonement of Jesus Christ to be unlocked fully*. Because of what Joseph saw and what began at this moment, the Savior was able, through this great and valiant servant and through others He sent, to restore power and privilege. That power and privilege allow us, and all who will live, to have the benefit of Jesus Christ's Atonement work in our lives."[8]

This significant truth—that salvation is in Christ—was not new to the world of 1820 and was, of course, central to what Christian churches of the day taught. But it stood as a confirming witness to the truth of the New Testament. In our day, at a time when so many people, young and old, have chosen to leave the Christian fold, this truth is needed even more now than it was in Joseph's day. Indeed, one of the principal functions of Restoration scripture is to testify of the essential truthfulness of the Bible (see 1 Nephi 13:39–40).

9. God the Father has form, shape, and identity. The fourteen-year-old Joseph "learned for [himself]" (Joseph Smith–History 1:20) that God our Heavenly Father is a man, a he, a person, and that we are created in his image. Did the young prophet learn in his First Vision

that God the Father has a physical, corporeal body? He certainly may have done so, but he did not mention this specific detail in any of the contemporary accounts.

On the one hand is the possible conclusion that Joseph Smith did not fully understand the physical nature of God the Father as a result of the First Vision. And on the other is the possible conclusion that Joseph Smith *did* indeed learn in the Sacred Grove that God has a body.

First, let us consider the possibility that Joseph may not have fully understood the physical nature of God the Father. The Prophet's growth in knowledge and understanding was often incremental, as is that of all mortals, and his development in understanding was thereby accomplished precept upon precept. When he left the grove of trees in 1820, Joseph Smith Jr. certainly did not have the doctrinal grasp or spiritual maturity he would have when he died a martyr's death in Carthage some twenty-four years later.

The earliest reference now in our possession to a sermon by Joseph Smith on the corporeality of God was written on 5 January 1841. On that occasion William Clayton recorded the Prophet as saying, "That which is without body or parts is nothing. There is no other God in heaven but that God who has flesh and bones."[9] Six weeks later, "Joseph said concerning the Godhead [that] it was not as many imagined—three heads and but one body; he said the three were separate bodies."[10] On 9 March 1841 Joseph declared that "the Son had a tabernacle and so had the Father."[11] Finally, on 2 April 1843 in Ramus, Illinois, Brother Joseph delivered instructions on the matter that are the basis for Doctrine and Covenants 130:22–23: "The Father has a body of flesh and bones as tangible as man's; the Son also; but the Holy Ghost . . . is a personage of Spirit."[12]

Second, let us consider the possibility that Joseph Smith did indeed learn in the Sacred Grove that God has a body. It is fascinating that very early in his ministry (November and December 1830), while involved in his inspired translation of Genesis in the King James Version of the Bible, Joseph recorded the following, which is now part of the book of Moses: "This was the book of the generations of Adam, saying: In the day that God created man, in the likeness of God made he him; *in the image of his own body*, male and female created he them" (Moses 6:8–9; emphasis added). We just may discover one day that the doctrine of the corporeality of God was made known, and perhaps understood by some members of the Church, many years earlier than we may have supposed.

The late Professor Milton V. Backman Jr. brought to light years ago a description of the beliefs of the Latter-day Saints by a Protestant clergyman in Ohio. Truman Coe, a Presbyterian minister who had for four years lived among the Saints in Kirtland, published the following regarding the beliefs of the Latter-day Saints in the 11 August 1836 *Ohio Observer*: "They contend that the God worshipped by the Presbyterians and all other sectarians is no better than a wooden god. *They believe that the true God is a material being, composed of body and parts*; and that when the Creator formed Adam in his own image, he made him about the size and shape of God himself."[13] If a minister of another faith had learned by 1836 that the Latter-day Saints were teaching that God has a body, it is not inconceivable that such things were known by Joseph earlier, perhaps even from the Sacred Grove.

Elder Jeffrey R. Holland wrote: "Inasmuch as Jesus was created in the express image of His Father, this should be a firm reminder of the divine bodily form (that of a man) that characterizes the Father's

> "They contend that the God worshipped by the Presbyterians and all other sectarians is no better than a wooden god. They believe that the true God is a material being, composed of body and parts; and that when the Creator formed Adam in his own image, he made him about the size and shape of God himself."
> —Truman Coe, Presbyterian minister

appearance as well as the Son's. Indeed, one of the Father's principal names is 'Man of Holiness' (Moses 6:57), with Christ regularly being called *the Son of Man*."[14]

10. The Father and the Son are separate and distinct persons and distinct beings. Only eleven days before his death, Joseph stated, "I have always declared God to be a distinct personage, Jesus Christ a separate and distinct personage from God the Father, and that the Holy Ghost was a distinct personage and a Spirit: and these three constitute three distinct personages and three Gods."[15]

As Latter-day Saints, we go to great lengths to make it clear that we are not a part of Nicene or Trinitarian Christianity. We believe that the Father and the Son are separate and distinct personages, separate Beings, that they are not somehow fused mysteriously or intertwined ontologically into the same Being. And yet, our Heavenly Father and his Beloved Son are infinitely more one than they are separate. They happen to be separate in person and being, but they are one in glory, one in purpose, one in focus and mission, and one in the sense that they both possess all of the attributes of godliness in perfection.[16] The brethren in the School of the Elders were taught in the winter of 1834–35 that the Father and the Son are one *in mind*, and that that oneness of mind is assured and maintained through the indwelling presence of the Holy Spirit. The Father and the Son possess "the same mind, the same wisdom, glory, power, and fullness—filling all in all; the Son being filled with the fullness of the mind, glory, and power; or, in other words, the spirit, glory, and power, of the Father."[17]

"We believe these three divine persons constituting a single Godhead are united in purpose, in manner, in testimony, in mission," explained Elder Jeffrey R. Holland. "We believe Them to be filled with the same godly sense of mercy and love, justice and grace, patience, forgiveness, and redemption. I think it is accurate to say we believe They are one in every significant and eternal aspect *except* believing Them to be three persons combined in one substance, a Trinitarian notion never set forth in the scriptures because it is not true."[18]

11. God the Eternal Father operates through his Only Begotten Son, who is our Mediator, our Intercessor with the Father. All revelation since the Fall has come to us by and through Jehovah, who is Jesus Christ, and when the Father does appear, it is to introduce and bear record of the Son.[19] In short, there is order in the kingdom of God.

12. The Lord would soon begin a grand restoration, what the apostle Peter had called a "restitution of all things" (Acts 3:21), a new dispensation in which, as the apostle Paul had stated, God would "gather together in one all things in Christ, both which are in heaven, and which are on earth, even in him" (Ephesians 1:10). Joseph recorded: "They [the first two members of the Godhead] told me that all religious denominations were believing in incorrect doctrines, and that none of them was acknowledged of God as his church and kingdom. And I was expressly commanded to 'go not after them,' at the same time receiving a promise *that the fulness of the gospel should at some future time be made known unto me.*"[20]

The long-promised "restitution of all things" spoken of by the apostle Peter (Acts 3:19–21) was about to begin, and young Joseph was informed that he would be the Lord's instrument on earth to put that restitution into effect.

13. The heavens are not closed. God delights in those who seek after him and blesses them accordingly. In a letter to his uncle Silas Smith in 1833, Joseph wrote of the need for continual direction through prophets: "I have no doubt but that the holy prophets and apostles and saints in ancient days were saved in the kingdom of God. . . . [But] will all this purchase an assurance for me, or waft me to the regions of Eternal day with my garments spotless, pure, and white? Or, must I not rather obtain for myself, by my own faith and diligence, in keeping the commandments of the Lord, an assurance of salvation for

myself? And have I not an equal privilege with the ancient saints? And will not the Lord hear my prayers, and listen to my cries, as soon [as] he ever did to theirs if I come to him in the manner they did? Or is he a respecter of persons?"[21]

Latter-day Saints are aware that individuals throughout the earth who are not of our faith seek to know the will of the Almighty, so that they might carry it out. They strive to be guided and led by his Holy Spirit, and we believe that to the extent that they are true to the light they possess, they receive the Lord's heavenly help. God loves all of his children and is no respecter of persons (Acts 10:34). In saying that the heavens are no longer sealed, we mean that institutional revelation, revelation needed to guide the Church of Jesus Christ through apostles and prophets, has been restored. And of course those who receive and enjoy the comfort and inspiration of the Holy Spirit are entitled to divine guidance, individual and personal revelation.

> In saying that the heavens are no longer sealed, we mean that institutional revelation, revelation needed to guide the Church of Jesus Christ through apostles and prophets, has been restored. And of course those who receive and enjoy the comfort and inspiration of the Holy Spirit are entitled to divine guidance, individual and personal revelation.

14. Because it is life eternal to know God, the First Vision represents the beginning of the re-revelation of God, the Godhead, and the plan of salvation. Such truths concerning Deity are not simply fascinating theological points of discussion; they are sacred, saving truths, because they are inextricably linked to how salvation comes and from whom immortality and eternal life are gained (Moses 1:39). Elder B. H. Roberts put it simply: "There is nothing in our doctrines on Deity today . . . but was germinally present in that first great revelation" we know as the First Vision.[22]

15. God the Eternal Father and his Son, Jesus Christ, knew young

Joseph Smith Jr. by name, and they know you and me, as well. We are the spirit children of Almighty Elohim and lived with him for eons and ages before this earth was formed. We were raised, as it were, in a family, we there knew God, and he knew us. God's infinity precludes neither his immediacy nor his intimacy. He is as close to us as we will allow him to be.

It has often crossed my mind that the Father and the Son are in the business of people, for as Moses learned from God, "This is my work and my glory—to bring to pass the immortality and eternal life of man" (Moses 1:39). "God not only numbers the stars and knows their names," Elder Neal A. Maxwell taught, "but, more importantly, He knows us and our names, and He can heal our hearts and treat our wounds. Though wide-eyed with wonder, we, being His spirit children, are not aliens in His universe."[23] Elder Dieter F. Uchtdorf taught a profound truth: "While we may look at the vast expanse of the universe and say, 'What is man in comparison to the glory of creation?' God Himself said we are the reason He created the universe! . . . This is a paradox of man: compared to God, man is nothing; yet we are everything to God."[24]

> God's infinity precludes neither his immediacy nor his intimacy. He is as close to us as we will allow him to be.

• • •

I am certain that the preceding list is but a beginning of what we know and understand as a result of the First Vision, the theophany in Palmyra. We should supplement this list of great truths that have come into the world as a result of a fourteen-year-old's quest for forgiveness of his sins and an earnest desire to know which church he should join.

In his closing address at the October 2019 general conference, President Russell M. Nelson reminded the Saints that "in the springtime of the year 2020, it will be exactly 200 years since Joseph Smith experienced the theophany we know as the First Vision. God the Father and His Beloved Son, Jesus Christ, appeared to Joseph, a 14-year-old youth. *That event marked the onset of the Restoration of the gospel of Jesus Christ in its fulness, precisely as foretold in the Holy Bible.* Then came a succession of visits from heavenly messengers. . . . Each brought divine authority to bless God's children on earth once again."[25]

In speaking of the Savior in the grove, Joseph wrote: "He again forbade me to join with any" of the existing churches—and now attend to what follows— "and *many other things did he say unto me, which I cannot write at this time*" (Joseph Smith–History 1:20; emphasis added). How expansive that statement is! There were no doubt so many things that our Heavenly Father and his Son, Jesus Christ, wanted to make known to Joseph. In time the young prophet would come to know, line upon line and precept upon precept, all about the following:

- Receiving, translating, and publishing the Book of Mormon.
- Being ordained to the Aaronic and Melchizedek Priesthoods.
- Organizing the restored Church.
- Receiving scores of revelations.
- Undertaking an inspired translation of the King James Bible.
- Learning of Zion and dedicating the ground of its center place.
- Implementing the law of consecration and stewardship.
- Translating the book of Abraham.
- Organizing the quorums of the Aaronic and Melchizedek Priesthoods.
- Putting in place the Quorum of the First Presidency, the Quorum of the Twelve Apostles, and the Quorums of Seventy.
- Building and dedicating the Kirtland Temple.
- Receiving sacred keys in that temple.
- Delighting in a Pentecostal season in the period surrounding the temple's dedication.
- Learning and teaching what becomes of us at death.

- Coming to understand the doctrine and practices associated with the redemption of the dead.
- Introducing the temple endowment.
- Exercising the sealing power to bind husbands and wives, parents and children, together everlastingly.

And on and on. When Joseph Smith Jr. emerged from the Sacred Grove, that young and absolutely inexperienced fourteen-year-old boy would proceed to carry out and put into effect what would be a monumental work—the work of restoration, the reestablishment of the Church of Jesus Christ and the kingdom of God on earth.

Chapter 9

FORMATIVE AND FOUNDATIONAL TO OUR FAITH

"Joseph did not understand at the time the full import of the First Vision," Elder John A. Widtsoe pointed out, "but he treasured it and its message in his mind. As he approached maturity, *it became the foundation fact upon which his work was built. His later career was but an amplification of the truths revealed in the First Vision.*" Elder Widtsoe made one other keen observation: "He joined no church. The Palmyra revivalists were unsuccessful as far as he was concerned. Instead, had men only understood, *the First Vision of the boy was the biggest event connected with the revival.*"[1] President David O. McKay declared: "The appearing of the Father and the Son to Joseph Smith is the foundation of this Church. Therein lies the secret of its strength and vitality. This is true, and I bear witness to it. That one revelation answers all the queries of science regarding God and his divine personality. Don't you see what that means? What God is, is answered. His relation to his children is clear. His interest in humanity through authority delegated to man is apparent. The future of the work is assured. These and other glorious truths are clarified by that glorious first vision."[2]

That sacred appearance, that vision-visitation in Palmyra, is the starting point, the foundation on which the Restoration is built. It is the beginning of the revelation of God to humankind in these last days. It is a time foreseen by holy men and women for generations and centuries (see, for example, 2 Nephi 3:6–15; Mormon 8:16, 25; Moses 7:62).

JOSEPH SMITH: A SPECIAL WITNESS OF CHRIST

From the time fourteen-year-old Joseph Smith Jr. heard in 1820 the voice of the Almighty declaring that Jesus Christ is the Son of God to the time that the choice seer died as a martyr in Carthage Jail in 1844, Joseph bore the responsibility to bear witness of Jesus Christ, the Son of the Eternal Father. As the senior apostle of God on earth, he was under covenant to serve as a "special [witness] of the name of Christ in all the world" (Doctrine and Covenants 107:23). Of all the burdens upon his shoulders, not one pressed upon him more than the need to testify of the Savior, for as the angel declared to John the Beloved, "the testimony of Jesus is the spirit of prophecy" (Revelation 19:10).

Joseph Smith was and is a prophet of God, the head of the dispensation of the fulness of times, the "choice seer" foreseen by the ancients (2 Nephi 3:7). We revere him and are endlessly grateful for the life he lived, the sufferings he endured for the truth's sake, and the divine authority and doctrine that came to and through him. But we do not worship him. Our worship is reserved for God the Eternal Father and his Son, Jesus Christ. Joseph Smith understood only too well that he but walked in the shadow of our Lord and Savior. Hence the greatest accomplishment of Brother Joseph was to point the people of the Restoration toward and rivet them to the atoning work of the Son of God. There should never be any doubt about the ultimate object of our worship and adoration and our ultimate loyalty to him: our Savior, Jesus Christ.

In an address to BYU–Hawaii students, historian Richard L. Bushman stated that one reason some Latter-day Saints find themselves in the midst of a faith crisis is that they have constructed their foundation of faith upon someone or something other than the Lord Jesus

Christ. Thus when matters in Church history prove to be challenging to them, they not only slide away from The Church of Jesus Christ of Latter-day Saints but, in some cases, slide away from the Savior himself. "When this new information builds up, they grow concerned. Could it all be wrong?" Bushman said that when he has counseled with troubled Saints, "I have taken to asking the doubters a question. 'How do you feel about Jesus Christ?'" He continued: "Those who lose faith in Christ because they have lost faith in Joseph Smith have things backward. Joseph's mission was to increase faith in Christ, not in himself." Joseph would surely "want us to develop faith in [the Lord's] teachings, in Christ and the atonement, in prayer and adhesion to high moral standards, not in him as a man. He would want us to believe in the principles independent of the man [himself], as the Saints in the first decade did. We honor him as a prophet, to be sure, but as one who testified of the Savior. His revelations pointed beyond himself to Christ and the Father. I believe in Joseph Smith as a prophet of God, and most of you here today do too. But we must place our faith first in Christ, and believe in him apart from our faith in his messenger. Christ should be the anchor when we struggle and question." Moreover, Brother Bushman reminded us that "we now benefit from having not just one but many accounts of the First Vision, each one offering a different perspective. *The Vision is a powerful source of faith. . . . But we should keep in mind the Vision's purpose: it was to testify of the Lord.*"³

LOYALTY TO THE RESTORATION

We have emphasized that saving faith is in Christ the Lord, and our ultimate loyalty must be to him and to his Father. And yet loyalty is also due to the latter-day work that Jesus Christ set in motion through Joseph Smith.

President Gordon B. Hinckley observed that for more than two centuries "enemies, critics, and some would-be scholars have worn out their lives trying to disprove the validity of that vision. Of course they cannot understand it. . . . There had been nothing of comparable magnitude since the Son of God walked the earth in mortality. *Without it as a foundation stone of our faith and organization, we have nothing. With it, we have everything.*

"Much has been written, much will be written, in an effort to explain it away. The finite mind cannot comprehend it. But the testimony of the Holy Spirit, experienced by countless numbers of people all through the years since it happened, bears witness that it is true, that it happened as Joseph Smith said it happened, that it was as real as the sunrise over Palmyra, that it is an essential foundation stone, a cornerstone, without which the Church could not be 'fitly framed together' [Ephesians 2:19–21]."[4]

Many years ago while I was serving as the director of the institute of religion near Florida State University, the full-time missionaries dropped by. They did that quite regularly, usually to ask a question about some Church history or doctrinal matter. I invited them into my office, and the senior companion spoke for the two of them: "Brother Millet, we have a problem," he began. "We are teaching this terrific family here in Tallahassee who are really golden contacts. But they raised a question earlier this week. They are a Baptist family, and so they know their Bible well. We had spoken to them about eternal marriage and the eternal family. The father of the family said that there was a passage in the Bible that contradicted the idea of eternal marriage. He read the following to us: 'Jesus answered and said unto them [the Sadducees], Ye do err, not knowing the scriptures, nor the power of God. For in the resurrection they neither marry, not are given in marriage, but are as the angels of God in heaven' (Matthew 22:29–30)." The missionary paused and asked, "Brother Millet, did you know that the Bible teaches this?"

I nodded and answered that I did know about it. The elder then inquired, "Can you please give us a few scriptures that respond to those verses?" Again there was a brief pause, and he continued, "You know, passages from the Bible."

I replied quickly, "No, I cannot."

The other missionary followed up, "What do you mean you can't? Do you mean that you can't or that you won't?"

I answered, "I can't, and so I won't."

My answer startled them, and so the senior companion responded, "What do you mean you can't?"

I replied that I could not point out a biblical passage that speaks specifically of eternal marriage because there aren't any.

He asked nervously, "What do you mean when you say there aren't any? Don't we believe in eternal marriage?"

I indicated that yes, we did in fact believe in that sacred ordinance.

He continued, "Well, how can we believe in something that's not in the Bible?"

I looked from one of them to the other and said, "Elders, if everything taught by The Church of Jesus Christ of Latter-day Saints were in the Bible, we wouldn't need a Restoration. Do you see that?"

The senior companion shook his head back and forth, as if to clear it. Then he spoke out with more volume, "Oh, yes, I see that. That makes sense."

"Here's what you need to do," I suggested. "Sit down with the Brown family, bear your testimony that in these latter days God called a modern prophet, Joseph Smith, and revealed to him and his prophetic successors many wonderful truths that were once understood in the early Christian church but have since been lost. One of those is the covenant and ordinance that we know as the new and everlasting covenant of marriage, performed in holy temples by one holding proper authority. Then you need to read slowly to them from Doctrine and Covenants 132:15–20."

"Wait a minute, Brother Millet," the senior elder responded.

"The Browns are not going to accept anything in the Doctrine and Covenants."

"Then," I replied, "they may not at this point be as golden as you thought. You go back and bear witness of latter-day revelation and of living apostles and prophets. That is what we have to offer to God's children on earth; this is the contribution the Latter-day Saints can make to the religious world." They left my office, possibly seeing things from a different vantage point.

An incident in our Church's history illustrates the power of this principle of being up to date and thus being relevant in the world. Elder Parley P. Pratt wrote of an occasion in late 1839 on which the Prophet Joseph Smith and Sidney Rigdon addressed a large congregation in Philadelphia:

"While visiting with brother Joseph in Philadelphia, a very large church was opened for him to preach in, and about three thousand people assembled to hear him. Brother Rigdon spoke first, and dwelt on the Gospel, illustrating his doctrine by the Bible. When he was through, Brother Joseph arose like a lion about to roar; and being full of the Holy Ghost, spoke in great power, bearing testimony of the visions he had seen, the ministering of angels which he had enjoyed; and how he had found the plates of the Book of Mormon, and translated them by the gift and power of God. He commenced by saying: 'If nobody else had the courage to testify of so glorious a message from Heaven, and of the finding of so glorious a record, he felt to do it in justice to the people, and leave the event with God.'"[5]

This was no time to declare a message that any other minister from any other church might deliver. This was no occasion for sharing and seeking to establish doctrine from the Bible. Joseph's work was and is a new and independent revelation, his witness an independent witness. The result of Joseph Smith's sermon in Philadelphia?

Elder Pratt continued: "The entire congregation were astounded; electrified, as it were, and overwhelmed with the sense of the truth and power by which he spoke, and the wonders which he related. A lasting impression was made; many souls were gathered into the fold. And I bear witness," Brother Pratt concluded, "that he, by his faithful and powerful testimony, cleared his garments of their blood. Multitudes were baptized in Philadelphia and in the regions around."[6]

Clearly there is power, consummate power, in declaring the glad tidings of the restored gospel (see Doctrine and Covenants 31:1–4), in "bearing testimony to all the world of those things which are communicated unto [us]" (Doctrine and Covenants 84:61; compare 11:22; 42:12).[7]

POWER IN JOSEPH SMITH'S TESTIMONY

While I was serving as a young missionary in the Eastern States Mission, my companion and I moved into a small town in New Jersey, only to find that the local Protestant ministers had prepared their parishioners for our arrival. At almost every door we approached, we were met by a smiling face and the words, "Oh, you must be the Mormons. This is for you." They would then hand us an anti-Mormon tract or, in some cases, hold up their copy of a book by "countercultist" Walter Martin entitled *Kingdom of the Cults*. They would then indicate to us that our Church was one of the cults dealt with in the book. We saved the pamphlets, stacked them in the corner of the living room of the apartment, and soon had a rather substantial pile of material. Out of sheer curiosity we began to read the brochures during lunchtime. I can still recall the dark and empty feelings that filled my soul as we encountered question after question about selected doctrine and specific moments in the history of the Church. My senior companion was no different; he was as unsettled as I was.

For weeks we did our work, but our heart wasn't in it. We went through the motions but, without saying much to each other, sensed that we couldn't do this indefinitely. I broke the ice at lunch one afternoon with the rather brutal query: "Elder Johnson, what if the Church isn't true?"

He answered, "I don't know."

I followed up. "What if the Baptists are right?" (There was a strong contingent of Baptists in the area.)

He said, "I just don't know."

"What if the Catholics are right? What if they have had the authority all along?"

My companion responded, "I've been wondering the same thing." Then presumably in an effort to cheer me up, he asked, "Elder Millet, do you think we are doing anything wrong? I mean, even if we are not a part of the true church, are we hurting anyone?"

I sheepishly replied that we were probably not doing anything destructive.

"Then," he said, "maybe we should keep working."

I asked with much pain in my voice, "Is that supposed to make me feel better? If so, it doesn't."

He indicated that under the present circumstances it was the best he could do.

I am ashamed to admit that prior to this time I had never prayed intently about my testimony. I was raised in the Church. Mom and Dad had a testimony, and I knew that they knew. That always seemed adequate. But now I was up against the wall of faith, and suddenly what they knew did not seem sufficient to settle my troubled heart. I prayed and I pleaded. I begged the Lord for light, for help, for anything! These vexations of the soul went on for about a month. I had actually concluded (though I had not confided the same to my companion) that if relief were not forthcoming shortly, I would pack my bags and go home. It did not seem proper to be engaged seriously in a cause about which I could not bear testimony.

We returned home for lunch a few days later, and my companion set about the task of making the soup and preparing the peanut butter sandwiches. I collapsed in a large chair in the living room, removed my shoes, and loosened my tie. As I began to reflect once more on my testimony problem, my heart ached. My feelings were close to the surface, and I yearned for deliverance from my pain. For some reason I reached to a nearby lamp table and picked up a copy of the pamphlet *Joseph Smith Tells His Own Story*. I suppose I had read that pamphlet twenty times. I began reading the opening lines. I came to the Prophet's statement that he was born on 23 December 1805 in Sharon, Windsor County, Vermont, and I was suddenly and without warning immersed in the most comforting and soothing influence I had ever known. It seemed at the time as if I were being wrapped in a large blanket as I began to be filled with the warmth of the Holy Spirit from head to toe. I wept as the spirit of confusion departed and the spirit of conversion encompassed me, and as I came to know assuredly that what we were doing was right and true and good. I did not hear specific words, but my feelings on that occasion were, "Of course it's true. You know that now, and you've known it for a long time." Another feeling was to the effect that the answers to what was troubling me were for the time being beyond my present capacity to comprehend. In time the answers would come, answers that would be as satisfying to the mind as they were soothing to the heart. The answers came, in fact, within months, and I marveled then how something so simple could have been so problematic before.

The Spirit touched my heart and told me things my mind did not yet understand. I was then in a position to proceed confidently with my work until my head caught up with my heart. Formerly I was in agony, was not at peace, and was subject to the nagging and uncomfortable power of doubt and uncertainty. Afterwards I was at peace, at rest, secure in the knowledge that my faith was well founded. The simple words of Joseph Smith's testimony—words from his official (1838) account—went into my heart and burned like fire. They changed my life. In looking back on that experience, I am reminded of the words of President Harold B. Lee. A person is converted, he taught, "when he sees with his eyes what he ought to see; when he hears with his ears what he ought to hear; and when he understands with his heart what he ought to understand. And what he ought to see, hear, and understand is truth—eternal truth—and then practice it. That is conversion."[8]

Several years ago, two full-time missionaries assigned to our stake in Orem, Utah, were invited to speak in our sacrament meeting. The first to address the congregation was a very new, inexperienced, and obviously frightened young elder. He stood before us for about thirty seconds silently as he waited (and prayed, I'm sure) for his nervousness to subside. He then opened his mouth and told us who he was and where he was from. At that point, the young elder said, essentially, "I want to say a few words about the Prophet Joseph Smith." After another brief pause—during which I sensed that many in the congregation were praying for him—he stood erect and began to tell the story of Joseph Smith's First Vision. In fact, he quoted, word for word from Joseph Smith–History 1:10–20. I saw the Spirit of the Lord resting upon that young but bold servant of the Lord. It is impossible for me to describe the power of the Spirit that entered and filled that room. I was in tears, as was my wife, Shauna, and about half the congregation. He closed with, "I bear you my testimony that this really did happen. I know it." And we knew that he knew.

This occasion illustrated two essential points. First, there is power in quoting scripture, and Joseph Smith–History is holy scripture. Second, there is a spiritual presence, a distinctive endowment of power,

> There is a spiritual presence, a distinctive endowment of power, that attends the earnest reading or recitation of the story of Joseph Smith's First Vision. I believe this takes place because of the truthfulness of what Joseph declared, but also because of the power that accompanies that story.

that attends the earnest reading or recitation of the story of Joseph Smith's First Vision. I believe this takes place because of the truthfulness of what Joseph declared, but also because of the power that accompanies that story; it is a recitation of how this all got started, how God our Father chose in these last days to set things straight. It is the saga of how the dispensation of the fulness of times was ushered in. And one would suppose that such an outpouring of the Spirit simply ought to be associated with the greatest event in this world since the Resurrection of the Lord Jesus Christ.

Arthur Henry King, a British convert whose academic training was in linguistics, began teaching at Brigham Young University in 1971. There he inspired hundreds of students and faculty with his remarkable mind and spiritual sensitivity. Brother King stated that there were certain specific matters within Latter-day Saint teachings that attracted him. He remarked that Restoration teachings were "clear of gnosticism and, in particular, of the vicious belief . . . that spirit is good and flesh evil." He was also touched and stirred by a belief that our postmortal existence logically called for a belief in a premortal existence. After being married, he said, "I attended the LDS Crawley chapel in Sussex, England. We arranged for the missionaries to visit the house regularly. I am glad that the first thing they did was to give me the pamphlet on Joseph Smith's vision. The style of the Joseph Smith story immediately struck me. He spoke to me, as soon as I read his testimony, as a great writer, transparently sincere and matter-of-fact. That is what endeared him to me—so matter-of-fact. When Joseph Smith describes his visions, he describes them as not a man who feels that he has to make the effort to persuade. He simply states what happened to him, and he does it in a way that gives it credence. I am in this Church because of the Joseph Smith story; my fundamental act of faith was to accept this as a remarkable document."[9]

Do we appreciate that there is power in the word (Alma 31:5), especially the sobering but soul-satisfying word that a revolution called the Restoration is underway? Because of what took place in a grove of trees in upstate New York in 1820, nothing will ever be the same. Joseph Fielding McConkie stated the matter boldly: "Had Joseph Smith sought answers in the Bible, instead of on his knees in a quiet grove, we would still be waiting for the restoration of the gospel promised in the Bible. Similarly, in missionary work, as long as we attempt to show people the path of salvation as stemming from the Bible, we become nothing more than another of the squabbling sects of Christendom." Brother McConkie added, "The well-trained missionary," and that includes all of us who are reading this book, "will answer investigators' questions by finding the simplest and most direct route to the Sacred Grove."[10]

> "The well-trained missionary will answer investigators' questions by finding the simplest and most direct route to the Sacred Grove."
> —Joseph Fielding McConkie

As a recent convert to The Church of Jesus Christ of Latter-day Saints, Thomas B. Marsh was counseled by the Lord, "Lift up your heart and rejoice, for the hour of your mission is come; and your tongue shall be loosed, and you shall declare glad tidings of great joy unto this generation." What, specifically, was Brother Marsh to teach? What were the "glad tidings"? Was he to travel far and wide to preach the Savior's Sermon on the Mount? Was he to bear witness of and interpret the Lord's parables? No, the specific charge was to *"declare the things which have been revealed to my servant, Joseph Smith, Jun."* (Doctrine and Covenants 31:3–4; emphasis added).

On 8 August 1938 President J. Reuben Clark Jr. of the First Presidency of the Church, under assignment, delivered a message to professional religious educators that stands today as an inspired beacon and a constitution of sorts for the teaching and declaration of the principles and doctrine of the restored gospel. President Clark spoke of the sober responsibility of the gospel teacher but also the glorious task to which he or she has been appointed or called. "As teachers you stand upon the highest peak in education, for what teaching can compare in priceless value and in far-reaching effect with that which deals with man as he was in the eternity of yesterday, as he is in the mortality of today, and as he will be in the forever of tomorrow. Not only time but eternity is your field."[11]

And yet there are realities, certain inviolable truths to which the gospel teacher, and every member of the Church, for that matter, must subscribe and proclaim in standing before the Saints of the Most High. President Clark spoke of "two prime things that may not be overlooked, forgotten, shaded, or discarded."[12] The first of these, he said, is the divine reality that Jesus Christ is the Beloved Son of God, our Savior and Redeemer; the One who suffered and died for our sins; the one who rose from the dead in glorious immortality.

The second, President Clark said, is that "the Father and the Son actually and in truth and very deed appeared to the Prophet Joseph in a vision in the woods; that other heavenly visions followed to Joseph and to others; that the gospel and the Holy Priesthood after the Order of the Son of God were in truth and fact restored to the earth from which they were lost by the apostasy of the primitive Church; that the Lord again set up His Church, through the agency of Joseph Smith; that the Book of Mormon is just what it professes to be; that to the Prophet came numerous revelations for guidance, upbuilding, organization, and encouragement of the Church and its members; that the Prophet's successors, likewise called of God, have received revelations as the needs of the Church have required." President Clark added that "these facts . . . must stand, unchanged, unmodified,

> President Clark spoke of "two prime things that may not be overlooked, forgotten, shaded, or discarded." The first of these, he said, is the divine reality that Jesus Christ is the Beloved Son of God, our Savior and Redeemer.
> —President J. Reuben Clark Jr.

without dilution, excuse, apology, or avoidance; *they may not be explained away or submerged. Without these two great beliefs the Church would cease to be the Church.*"[13]

• • •

My grandfather Anatole J. Millet joined The Church of Jesus Christ of Latter-day Saints in the 1930s near New Orleans, Louisiana. He had been brought up as a Roman Catholic, and so when he left the faith of his parents, he was basically asked to leave their home. Later he and my grandmother raised their four sons as Latter-day Saints. By the time I was born, my father and mother were not extremely active church attenders, but in time they felt the need to bring up their children in the Church. Both of them went on to serve in responsible positions in the Church and set a noble and significant example for me and my siblings.

I was baptized when I was nine years of age. Not long after my baptism, I was asked to speak in sacrament meeting. My dad felt at that early stage of his spiritual reactivation that he was much less able to help me in preparing my message than was his older brother, my Uncle Joseph, who wrote my talk for me. I memorized it. It has now been more than sixty years since I looked out at that rather frightening congregation, delivered those halting words of a talk that couldn't have lasted more than four or five minutes, and then sat down with a feeling of overwhelming relief.

I also remember something else about that occasion—namely, how I felt at the time. Although I was terribly nervous and insecure behind the pulpit, I began on that occasion to feel the stirrings of testimony, the beginnings of a spiritual witness that what I was speaking about was true and that it had actually happened. I also felt that it was very important. The peace I felt as I sat down was not simply the flood of emotion associated with having completed a daunting task but was also the quiet and poignant assurance that I had spoken the truth. I knew something when I sat down that I had not known before I stood up to speak.

You see, my first talk as a Latter-day Saint was a very simple message about Joseph Smith's First Vision—the story of how young Joseph wrestled in 1820 with questions about which church to join, how he encountered varying and conflicting views on religious questions, and how he chose to follow the scriptural admonition to ask God for wisdom. In words appropriate to a nine-year-old, I bore a quiet and timid testimony of what took place in Palmyra, New York, nearly fourteen hundred miles from where I was standing, a theophany that occurred 136 years before I was born.

In the decades since that first talk, I have learned a great deal about Jacksonian America: the utopian and communitarian societies that began to spring up; the "Second Great Awakening" and many of its most prominent figures; the spirit of revivalism in the Northeastern United States; and the "Burned-Over District," so called because of the fires of revivalism that had swept the area. I have read and studied in great detail the life and work of Joseph Smith Jr. with passion and with zeal. I have consumed his revelations, translations, and sermons for the better part of my life, and they have become formative and foundational to my current walk and talk. They are now a part of me. And the simple but sincere testimony that I shared in the 1950s has been greatly added upon—expanded, broadened, and deepened. And God has been gracious to me in banishing from my mind and heart doubt or hesitation relative to the origins of the Restoration and the religious path I have taken.

I know that God our Heavenly Father lives, that he is the Father of our spirits, and that he has a body of flesh and bones. I know that Jesus of Nazareth was and is the Holy Messiah, the Anointed One, the Savior and Redeemer; that he has bought us with his blood; and that salvation comes by and through him and in no other way.

Now the same Spirit that witnesses to my soul of the reality and love and saving grace of the Father and the Son has also borne testimony to me of the truths of the Restoration. I know with certainty, as though I had been there in the Sacred Grove with him, that young Joseph Smith saw and heard just what he reported. God our Father and Jesus Christ, his Son, were there. The Spirit of the Lord has whispered to me again and again that the restored gospel is in very deed the restoration of first-century Christianity.

In essence, the voice of God has spoken to my mind and heart and beckoned, "This is the way, walk ye in it" (Isaiah 30:21). To do so faithfully and until the day I die is my earnest desire and my sacred ambition. May God bless us that we may recognize, acknowledge, and testify of the marvelous work and a wonder that began with Joseph Smith's First Vision.

Appendix

CONTEMPORARY ACCOUNTS OF THE FIRST VISION

Spelling and punctation for these accounts have been modernized.

JOSEPH SMITH'S 1832 ACCOUNT

A history of the life of Joseph Smith Jr., an account of his marvelous experience, and of all the mighty acts which he does in the name of Jesus Christ, the Son of the living God, of whom he bears record. And also an account of the rise of the Church of Christ in the eve of time, according as the Lord brought forth and established [it] by his hand. First, he received the testimony from on high; second, the ministering of angels; third, the reception of the holy priesthood by the ministering of angels, to administer the letter of the Gospel, the Law and commandments as they were given unto him, and the ordinances; fourth, a confirmation and reception of the High Priesthood after the holy order of the Son of the living God—power and ordinances from on high to preach the gospel in the administration and demonstration of the Spirit; the keys of the kingdom of God conferred upon him and the continuation of the blessings of God to him, etc.

I was born in the town of Sharon, in the State of Vermont, North America, on the twenty third day of December AD 1805, of goodly parents who spared no pains in instructing me in the Christian religion. At the age of about ten years, my father, Joseph Smith Senior, moved to Palmyra, Ontario County, in the state of New York. Being in indigent circumstances [we] were obliged to labor hard for the support of a large family, having nine children. As it required the exertions of all that were able to render any assistance for the support of the family, therefore we were deprived of the benefit of an education. Suffice it to say [that] I was merely instructed in reading ~~and~~ writing and the ground rules of arithmetic, which constituted my whole literary acquirements.

At about the age of twelve years, my mind became seriously impressed with regard to the all-important concerns for the welfare of my immortal soul, which led me to searching the scriptures, believing as I was taught, that they contained the word of God. Thus applying myself to them, and my intimate acquaintance with those of different denominations, led me to marvel exceedingly, for I discovered that they did not adorn their profession by a holy walk and Godly conversation, agreeable to what I found contained in that sacred depository. This was a grief to my soul. Thus from the age of twelve years to fifteen I pondered many things in my heart concerning the situation of the world of mankind, the contentions and divisions, the wickedness and abominations, and the darkness which pervaded the minds of mankind.

My mind become exceedingly distressed, for I became convicted of my sins, and by searching the scriptures I found that mankind did not come unto the Lord, but that they had apostatized from the true and living faith, and there was no society or denomination that built upon the gospel of Jesus Christ, as recorded in the New Testament. And I felt to mourn for my own sins and for the sins of the world, for I learned in the scriptures that God was the same yesterday, today, and forever, that he was no respecter to persons, for he was God.

I looked upon the sun, the glorious luminary of the earth, and also the moon rolling in their majesty through the heavens; and also the stars shining in their courses; and the earth also upon which I stood; and the beast of the field and the fowls of heaven; and the fish of the waters; and also man walking forth upon the face of the earth, in majesty and in the strength of beauty, whose power and intelligence in governing the things which are so exceeding great and marvelous, even in the likeness of him who created him. And when I considered upon these things, my heart exclaimed, "Well hath the wise man said, 'The fool saith in his heart, there is no God.'" My heart exclaimed, "All these bear testimony and bespeak an omnipotent and omnipresent power, a Being who makes laws and decrees and binds all things in their bounds, who fills eternity, who was and is and will be from all eternity to eternity."

And when I considered all these things and that that Being seeks such to worship him [and to] worship him in spirit and in truth, therefore I cried unto the Lord for mercy, for there was none else to whom I could go and obtain mercy, and the Lord heard my cry in the wilderness. While in the attitude of calling upon the Lord, in the 16th year of my age, a pillar of light above the brightness of the sun at noon day come down from above and rested upon me. I was filled with the Spirit of God, and the Lord opened the heavens upon me, and I saw the Lord and he spake unto me, saying, "Joseph, my son, thy sins are forgiven thee. Go thy way, walk in my statutes, and keep my commandments. Behold, I am the Lord of glory. I was crucified for the world, that all those who believe on my name may have eternal life. Behold, the world lies in sin at this time, and none doeth good, no, not one; they have turned aside from the gospel and keep not my commandments. They draw near to me with their lips, while their hearts are far from me. Mine anger is kindling against the inhabitants of the earth, to visit them according to their ungodliness, and to bring to pass that which hath been spoken by the mouth of the prophets and apostles. Behold and lo, I come quickly, as it is written of me in the cloud, clothed in the glory of my Father."

My soul was filled with love, and for many days I could rejoice with great joy, and the Lord was with me. But [I] could find none that would believe the heavenly vision. Nevertheless, I pondered these things in my heart.

JOSEPH SMITH'S 1835 ACCOUNT

After I had made some remarks concerning the Bible, I commenced giving him [Robert Matthias] a relation of the circumstances connected with the coming forth of the Book of Mormon, as follows: Being wrought up in my mind, respecting the subject of religion, and looking at the different systems taught the children of men, I knew not who was right and who was wrong. And I considered it of the first importance to be right in matters that involve eternal consequences. Being thus perplexed in mind, I retired to the silent grove and bowed down before the Lord, under a realizing sense that he had said (if the Bible be true), "Ask, and you shall receive; knock and it shall be opened; seek and you shall find." And again, "If any man lack wisdom, let him ask of God, who giveth to all men liberally and upbraideth not."

Information was what I most desired at this time, and with a fixed determination to obtain it, I called upon the Lord for the first time, in the place above stated. Or, in other words, I made a fruitless attempt to pray. My tongue seemed to be swollen in my mouth, so that I could not utter. I heard a noise behind me, like some person walking towards me. I strove again to pray, but could not. The noise of walking seemed to draw nearer. I sprang upon my feet and looked around, but saw no person or thing that was calculated to produce the noise of walking. I kneeled again. My mouth was opened and my tongue liberated, and I called on the Lord in mighty prayer.

A pillar of fire appeared above my head. It presently rested down upon me and filled me with joy unspeakable. A personage appeared in the midst of this pillar of flame, which was spread all around, and yet nothing consumed. Another personage soon appeared like unto the first. He said unto me, "Thy sins are forgiven thee." He testified unto me that Jesus Christ is the Son of God. I saw many angels in this vision. I was about 14 years old when I received this first communication.

JOSEPH SMITH'S 1838 ACCOUNT (JOSEPH SMITH—HISTORY 1:5–20)

Some time in the second year after our removal to Manchester, there was in the place where we lived an unusual excitement on the subject of religion. It commenced with the Methodists, but soon became general among all the sects in that region of country. Indeed, the whole district of country seemed affected by it, and great multitudes united themselves to the different religious parties, which created no small stir and division amongst the people, some crying, "Lo, here!" and others, "Lo, there!" Some were contending for the Methodist faith, some for the Presbyterian, and some for the Baptist.

For, notwithstanding the great love which the converts to these different faiths expressed at the time of their conversion, and the great zeal manifested by the respective clergy, who were active in getting up and promoting this extraordinary scene of religious feeling, in order to have everybody converted, as they were pleased to call it, let them join what sect they pleased; yet when the converts began to file off, some to one party and some to another, it was seen that the seemingly good feelings of both the priests and the converts were more pretended than real; for a scene of great confusion and bad feeling ensued—priest contending against priest, and convert against convert; so that all their good feelings one for another, if they ever had any, were entirely lost in a strife of words and a contest about opinions.

I was at this time in my fifteenth year. My father's family was proselyted to the Presbyterian faith, and four of them joined that church, namely, my mother, Lucy; my brothers Hyrum and Samuel Harrison; and my sister Sophronia.

During this time of great excitement my mind was called up to serious reflection and great uneasiness; but though my feelings were deep and often poignant, still I kept myself aloof from all these parties, though I attended their several meetings as often as occasion would permit. In process of time my mind became somewhat partial to the Methodist sect, and I felt some desire to be united with them; but so great were the confusion and strife among the different denominations, that it was impossible for a person young as I was, and so unacquainted with men and things, to come to any certain conclusion who was right and who was wrong.

My mind at times was greatly excited, the cry and tumult were so great and incessant. The Presbyterians were most decided against the Baptists and Methodists, and used all the powers of both reason and sophistry to prove their errors, or, at least, to make the people think they were in error. On the other hand, the Baptists and Methodists in their turn were equally zealous in endeavoring to establish their own tenets and disprove all others.

In the midst of this war of words and tumult of opinions, I often said to myself: What is to be done? Who of all these parties are right; or, are they all wrong together? If any one of them be right, which is it, and how shall I know it?

While I was laboring under the extreme difficulties caused by the contests of these parties of religionists, I was one day reading the Epistle of James, first chapter and fifth verse, which reads: *If any of you lack wisdom, let him ask of God, that giveth to all men liberally, and upbraideth not; and it shall be given him.*

Never did any passage of scripture come with more power to the heart of man than this did at this time to mine. It seemed to enter with great force into every feeling of my heart. I reflected on it again and again, knowing that if any person needed wisdom from God, I did; for how to act I did not know, and unless I could get more wisdom than I then had, I would never know; for the teachers of religion of the different sects understood the same passages of scripture so differently as to destroy all confidence in settling the question by an appeal to the Bible.

At length I came to the conclusion that I must either remain in darkness and confusion, or else I must do as James directs, that is, ask of God. I at length came to the determination to "ask of God," concluding that if he gave wisdom to them that lacked wisdom, and would give liberally, and not upbraid, I might venture.

So, in accordance with this, my determination to ask of God, I retired to the woods to make the attempt. It was on the morning of a beautiful, clear day, early in the spring of eighteen hundred and twenty. It was the first time in my life that I had made such an attempt, for amidst all my anxieties I had never as yet made the attempt to pray vocally.

After I had retired to the place where I had previously designed to go, having looked around me, and finding myself alone, I kneeled down and began to offer up the desires of my heart to God. I had scarcely done so, when immediately I was seized upon by some power which entirely overcame me, and had such an astonishing influence over me as to bind my tongue so that I could not speak. Thick darkness gathered around me, and it seemed to me for a time as if I were doomed to sudden destruction.

But, exerting all my powers to call upon God to deliver me out of the power of this enemy which had seized upon me, and at the very moment when I was ready to sink into despair and abandon myself to destruction—not to an imaginary ruin, but to the power of some actual being from the unseen world, who had such marvelous power as I had never before felt in any being—just at this moment of great alarm, I saw a pillar of light exactly over my head, above the brightness of the sun, which descended gradually until it fell upon me.

It no sooner appeared than I found myself delivered from the enemy which held me bound. When the light rested upon me I saw two Personages, whose brightness and glory defy all description, standing above me in the air. One of them spake unto me, calling me by name and said, pointing to the other—*This is My Beloved Son. Hear Him!*

My object in going to inquire of the Lord was to know which of all the sects was right, that I might know which to join. No sooner, therefore, did I get possession of myself, so as to be able to speak, than I asked the Personages who stood above me in the light, which of all the sects was right (for at this time it had never entered into my heart that all were wrong)—and which I should join.

I was answered that I must join none of them, for they were all wrong; and the Personage who addressed me said that all their creeds were an abomination in his sight; that those professors were all corrupt; that: "they draw near to me with their lips, but their hearts are far from me, they teach for doctrines the commandments of men, having a form of godliness, but they deny the power thereof."

He again forbade me to join with any of them; and many other things did he say unto me, which I cannot write at this time. When I came to myself again, I found myself lying on my back, looking up into heaven. When the light had departed, I had no strength; but soon recovering in some degree, I went home. And as I leaned up to the fireplace, mother inquired what the matter was. I replied, "Never mind, all is well—I am well enough off." I then said to my mother, "I have learned for myself that Presbyterianism is not true." It seems as though the adversary was aware, at a very early period of my life, that I was destined to prove a disturber and an annoyer of his kingdom; else why should the powers of darkness combine against me? Why the opposition and persecution that arose against me, almost in my infancy?

ORSON PRATT'S 1840 ACCOUNT

When somewhere about fourteen or fifteen years old, he [Joseph Smith] began seriously to reflect upon the necessity of being prepared for a future state of existence: but how, or in what way, to prepare himself, was a question, as yet, undetermined in his own mind: he perceived that it was a question of infinite importance, and that the salvation of his soul depended upon a correct understanding of the same. He saw, that if he understood not the way, it would be impossible to walk in it, except by chance; and the thought of resting his hopes of eternal life upon chance, or uncertainties, was more than he could endure.

If he went to the religious denominations to seek information, each one pointed to its particular tenets, saying—"This is the way, walk ye in it;" while, at the same time, the doctrines of each were, in many respects, in direct opposition to one another. It also occurred to his mind, that God was not the author of but one doctrine, and therefore could not acknowledge but one denomination as his church, and that such denomination must be a people who believe and teach that one doctrine (whatever it may be) and build upon the same. He then reflected upon the immense number of doctrines now in the world, which had given rise to many hundreds of different denominations.

The great question to be decided in his mind, was—if any one of these denominations be the Church of Christ, which one is it? Until he could become satisfied in relation to this question, he could not rest contented. To trust to the decisions of fallible man, and build his hopes upon the same, without any certainty and knowledge of his own, would not satisfy the anxious desires that pervaded his breast. To decide, without any positive and definite evidence, on which he could rely, upon a subject involving the future welfare of his soul, was revolting to his feelings. The only alternative, that seemed to be left him, was to read the Scriptures, and endeavor to follow their directions.

He accordingly commenced perusing the sacred pages of the Bible with sincerity, believing the things that he read. His mind soon caught hold of the following passage: "If any of you lack wisdom, let him ask of God, that giveth to all men liberally, and upbraideth not; and it shall be given him" (James 1:5). From this promise he learned that it was the privilege of all men to ask God for wisdom, with the sure and certain expectation of receiving liberally, without being upbraided for so doing. This was cheering information to him: tidings that gave him great joy. It was like a light shining forth in a dark place, to guide him to the path in which he should walk. He now saw that if he inquired of God, there was not only a possibility but a probability; yea, more, a certainty, that he should obtain a knowledge, which, of all the doctrines, was the doctrine of Christ; and, which, of all the churches, was the church of Christ.

He therefore retired to a secret place in a grove, but a short distance from his father's house, and knelt down and began to call upon the Lord. At first, he was severely tempted by the powers of darkness, which endeavored to overcome him. But he continued to seek for deliverance, until darkness gave way from his mind, and he was enabled to pray in fervency of the spirit and in faith. And while thus pouring out his soul, anxiously desiring an answer from God, he at length saw a very bright and glorious light in the heavens above, which, at first, seemed to be at a considerable distance. He continued praying, while the light appeared to be gradually descending towards him; and, as it drew nearer, it increased in brightness and magnitude, so that by the time that it reached the tops of the trees, the whole wilderness, for some distance around, was illuminated in a most glorious and brilliant manner. He expected to have seen the leaves and boughs of the trees consumed, as soon as the light came in contact with them; but, perceiving that it did not produce that effect, he was encouraged with the hopes of being able to endure its presence.

It continued descending, slowly, until it rested upon the earth, and he was enveloped in the midst of it. When it first came upon him, it produced a peculiar sensation throughout his whole system, and immediately his mind was caught away from the natural objects with which he was surrounded, and he was enwrapped in a heavenly vision, and saw two glorious personages, who exactly resembled each other in their features or likeness.

He was informed that his sins were forgiven. He was also informed upon the subjects which had for some time previously agitated his mind—that all the religious denominations were believing in incorrect doctrines, and consequently that none of them was acknowledged of God as his church and kingdom. And he was expressly commanded to go not after them. And he received a promise that the true doctrine—the fulness of the gospel—should, at some future time, be made known to him, after which the vision withdrew, leaving his mind in a state of calmness and peace indescribable.

ORSON HYDE'S 1842 ACCOUNT

When he [Joseph Smith] had reached his fifteenth year, he began to think seriously about the importance of preparing for a future [existence]; but it was very difficult for him to decide how he should go about such an important undertaking. He recognized clearly that it would be impossible for him to walk the proper path without being acquainted with it beforehand; and to base his hopes for eternal life on chance or blind uncertainty would have been more than he had ever been inclined to do.

He discovered the world of religion working under a flood of errors, which, by virtue of their contradictory opinions and principles, laid the foundation for the rise of such different sects and denominations whose feelings toward each other all too often were poisoned by hate, contention, resentment and anger. He felt that there was only one truth, and that those who understood it correctly all understood it in the same way. Nature had endowed him with a keen critical intellect, and so he looked through the lens of reason and common sense and with pity and contempt upon those systems of religion, which were so opposed to each other and yet were all obviously based on the scriptures.

After he had sufficiently convinced himself to his own satisfaction that darkness covered the earth and gross darkness [covered] the nations, the hope of ever finding a sect or denomination that was in possession of unadulterated truth left him.

Consequently he began in an attitude of faith his own investigation of the word of God [feeling that it was] the best way to arrive at a knowledge of the truth. He had not proceeded very far in this laudable endeavor when his eyes fell upon the following verse of St. James (1:5): "If any of you lack wisdom, let him ask of God, that giveth to all men liberally, and upbraideth not; and it shall be given him." He considered this scripture an authorization for him to solemnly call upon his creator, to present his needs before him with the certain expectation of some success. And so he began to pour out to the Lord with fervent determination the earnest desires of his soul.

On one occasion, he went to a small grove of trees near his father's home and knelt down before God in solemn prayer. The adversary then made several strenuous efforts to cool his ardent soul. He filled his mind with doubts and brought to mind all manner of inappropriate images to prevent him from obtaining the object of his endeavors. But the overflowing mercy of God came to buoy him up and gave new impetus to his failing strength. However, the dark cloud soon parted and light and peace filled his frightened heart. Once again he called upon the Lord with faith and fervency of spirit.

At this sacred moment, the natural world around him was excluded from his view, so that he would be open to the presentation of heavenly and spiritual things. Two glorious heavenly personages stood before him, resembling each other exactly in features and stature. They told him that his prayers had been answered and that the Lord had decided to grant him a special blessing. He was also told that he should not join any of the religious sects or denominations, because all of them erred in doctrine and none was recognized by God as his church and kingdom. He was further commanded to wait patiently until some future time, when the true doctrine of Christ and the complete truth of the gospel would be revealed to him. The vision closed and peace and calm filled his mind.

JOSEPH SMITH'S 1842 ACCOUNT (WENTWORTH LETTER)

When about fourteen years of age, I began to reflect upon the importance of being prepared for a future state, and upon enquiring about the plan of salvation, I found that there was a great clash in religious sentiment; if I went to one society, they referred me to one plan, and another to another, each one pointing to his own particular creed as the *summum bonum* of perfection. Considering that all could not be right, and that God could not be the author of so much confusion, I determined to investigate the subject more fully, believing that if God had a church it would not be split up into factions, and that if he taught one society to worship one way, and administer in one set of ordinances, he would not teach another principles which were diametrically opposed.

Believing the word of God, I had confidence in the declaration of James; "If any man lack wisdom, let him ask of God, who giveth to all men liberally and upbraideth not, and it shall be given him." I retired to a secret place in a grove and began to call upon the Lord. While fervently engaged in supplication, my mind was taken away from the objects with which I was surrounded, and I was enwrapped in a heavenly vision and saw two glorious personages who exactly resembled each other in features and likeness, surrounded with a brilliant light which eclipsed the sun at noonday. They told me that all religious denominations were believing in incorrect doctrines and that none of them was acknowledged of God as his church and kingdom. And I was expressly commanded to "go not after them," at the same time receiving a promise that the fulness of the gospel should at some future time be made known unto me.

DAVID NYE WHITE'S 1843 ACCOUNT

The Lord does reveal himself to me. I know it. He revealed himself first to me when I was about fourteen years old, a mere boy. I will tell you about it. There was a reformation among the different religious denominations in the neighborhood where I lived, and I became serious, and was desirous to know which church to join. While thinking of this matter, I opened the [New] Testament promiscuously on these words, in James: "Ask of the Lord, who giveth to all men liberally and upbraideth not." I just determined I'd ask him.

I immediately went out into the woods, where my father had a clearing, and went to the stump where I had stuck my axe when I had quit work. And I kneeled down, and prayed, saying, "O Lord, what church shall I join?" Directly I saw a light, and then a glorious personage in the light, and then another personage, and the first personage said [of] the second, "Behold, my beloved Son, hear him." I then addressed this second person, saying, "O Lord, what church shall I join?" He replied, "Don't join any of them; they are all corrupt." The vision then vanished, and when I came to myself, I was sprawling on my back, and it was some time before my strength returned.

When I went home and told the people I had a revelation, and that all the churches were corrupt, they persecuted me, and they have persecuted me ever since. They thought to put me down, but they haven't succeeded, and they can't do it.

ALEXANDER NEIBAUR'S 1844 ACCOUNT

Brother Joseph told us [of] the first call he had. [At a] revival meeting, his mother and brother and sister got religion. He wanted to get religion, too, and wanted to feel and shout like the rest, but could feel nothing.

He opened his Bible, and the first passage that struck him was, "If any man lacks wisdom, let him ask of God, who giveth to all men liberally and upbraideth not." He went into the woods to pray and knelt himself down. His tongue was cleaved to the roof [of his mouth]; he could not utter a word. He felt easier after a while. He saw a fire towards heaven that came nearer and nearer. He saw a personage in the fire, [who had] a light complexion and blue eyes. A piece of white cloth was drawn over his shoulders, and his right arm was bare. After a while another person came to the side of the first. Mr. Smith then asked, "Must I join the Methodist Church?" [He was told] "No, they are not my people. All have gone astray. There is none that doeth good, no, not one. But this is my beloved Son; hearken ye to him." The fire drew nearer and rested upon the trees. It enveloped and comforted him.

He endeavored to rise, but felt uncommonly feeble. He got into [his] house. He told the Methodist priest [about his vision], who said that this was not an age for God to reveal himself in visions. Revelation had ceased with the New Testament.

SOURCES

Allen, James B. "Emergence of a Fundamental: The Expanding Role of Joseph Smith's First Vision in Mormon Religious Thought." *Journal of Mormon History* 7 (1980): 43–61.

Allen, James B., and John W. Welch. "The Appearance of the Father and the Son to Joseph Smith in 1820." In *Exploring the First Vision*, edited by Samuel Alonzo Dodge and Steven C. Harper. Provo, UT: Brigham Young University Religious Studies Center, 2012.

Andersen, Neil L. *The Divine Gift of Forgiveness*. Salt Lake City: Deseret Book, 2019.

Anderson, Richard Lloyd. "Parallel Prophets: Paul and Joseph Smith." *Brigham Young University Fireside and Devotional Speeches*. Provo, UT: Brigham Young University Publications, 1983, speeches.byu.edu.

Andrus, Hyrum L., and Helen Mae Andrus, eds. *They Knew the Prophet*. Salt Lake City: Bookcraft, 1974.

Asay, Carlos E. "'Oh, How Lovely Was the Morning!': Joseph Smith's First Prayer and the First Vision." *Ensign*, April 1995.

Ayto, John. *Dictionary of Word Origins*. London: A & C Black, 2005.

Backman, Milton V., Jr. *American Religions and the Rise of Mormonism*. Rev. ed. Salt Lake City: Deseret Book, 1970.

———. "Awakenings in the Burned-Over District: New Light on the Historical Setting of the First Vision." *Brigham Young University Studies* 9, no. 3 (1969): 301–20, scholarsarchive.byu.edu.

———. *Joseph Smith's First Vision*. 2nd ed. Salt Lake City: Bookcraft, 1980.

———. "Truman Coe's 1836 Description of Mormonism." *Brigham Young University Studies* 17, no. 3 (1977): 347, 354, scholarsarchive.byu.edu.

Ballard, M. Russell. "The Miracle of the Holy Bible." *Ensign*, May 2007.

Balmer, Randall. *Mine Eyes Have Seen the Glory: A Journey into the Evangelical Subculture in America*. 3rd ed. New York: Oxford University Press, 2000.

Bangerter, W. Grant. "It's a Two-Way Street." *Brigham Young University 1984–85 Devotional and Fireside Speeches*. Provo, UT: Brigham Young University Publications, 1985, speeches.byu.edu.

Baugh, Alexander L. "Joseph Smith: Seer, Translator, Revelator, and Prophet." Brigham Young University devotional address, 24 June 2014, speeches.byu.edu.

Bednar, David A. "Ask in Faith." *Ensign*, May 2008.

Benson, Ezra Taft. "Born of God." *Ensign*, November 1985.

———. "Civic Standards for the Faithful Saints." *Ensign*, July 1972.

———. *Ezra Taft Benson* [manual]. In *Teachings of Presidents of the Church* series. Salt Lake City: The Church of Jesus Christ of Latter-day Saints, 2014.

———. *God, Family, Country: Our Three Great Loyalties*. Salt Lake City: Deseret Book, 1974.

Berrett, William E., and Alma P. Burton. *Readings in L.D.S. Church History*. 3 vols. Salt Lake City: Deseret Book, 1953.

Briggs, E. C., and J. W. Peterson Interview. *Deseret News*, 20 January 1894.

Brown, Matthew B. *A Pillar of Light: The History and Message of the First Vision*. Salt Lake City: Covenant Communications, 2009.

Bushman, Richard Lyman. *A Believing History: Latter-day Saint Essays*. Edited by Reid L. Neilson and Jed Woodworth. New York: Columbia University Press, 2004.

———. "A Joseph Smith for the Twenty-First Century." *Brigham Young University Studies* 40, no. 3 (2001): 155–71, scholarsarchive.byu.edu.

———. *Joseph Smith, Rough Stone Rolling: A Cultural Biography of Mormonism's Founder*. New York: Alfred A. Knopf, 2005.

———. "The Visionary World of Joseph Smith." *Brigham Young University Studies* 37, no. 1 (1997): 183–204, scholarsarchive.byu.edu.

Butler, Jon, Grant Wacker, and Randall Balmer. *Religion in American Life: A Short History*. New York: Oxford University Press, 2003.

Callister, Tad R. *The Inevitable Apostasy and the Promised Restoration*. Salt Lake City: Deseret Book, 2006.

Campbell, Alexander. *The Christian Baptist*. Revised by D. S. Burnet. 7 vols. 13th ed. Bethany, WV: H. S. Bosworth, 1861.

Campbell, William W. *The Life and Writings of DeWitt Clinton*. New York: Baker and Scribner, 1849.

Cannon, George Q. *Gospel Truth: Discourses and Writings of George Q. Cannon*. 2 vols. in 1. Salt Lake City: Deseret Book, 1987.

———. *Life of Joseph Smith the Prophet*. Salt Lake City: Deseret Book, 1972.

Cartwright, Peter. *The Backwoods Preacher: Autobiography of Peter Cartwright*. London: Arthur Hall, Virtue, and Co., 1862.

Christensen, Matthew B. *The First Vision: A Harmonization of 10 Accounts from the Sacred Grove*. Springville, UT: Cedar Fort, 2014.

Clark, J. Reuben, Jr. "The Charted Course of the Church in Education," churchofjesuschrist.org/bc/content/shared/content/english/pdf/language-materials/32709_eng.pdf?lang=eng. Or see *J. Reuben Clark: Selected Papers*, edited by David H. Yarn Jr. 5 vols. Provo, UT: Brigham Young University Press, 1984.

Cook, Quentin L. "Valiant in the Testimony of Jesus." *Ensign*, November 2016.

Cowley, Matthew. *Matthew Cowley Speaks*. Salt Lake City: Deseret Book, 1954.

Dodge, Samuel Alonzo, and Steven C. Harper, eds. *Exploring the First Vision*. Provo, UT: Brigham Young University Religious Studies Center, 2012.

Durant, Will, and Ariel Durant. *Caesar and Christ.* Vol. 3 in *The Story of Civilization.* 11 vols. New York: Simon & Schuster, 1935–75.
Encyclopedia of Mormonism. Edited by Daniel H. Ludlow, et al. 6 vols. New York: Macmillan, 1992.
Emerson, Ralph Waldo. "Harvard Divinity School Address," 15 July 1838. In *Theology in America,* edited by Sydney E. Ahlstrom. Indianapolis, IN: Bobbs-Merrill, 1967.
Eyring, Henry B. *Because He First Loved Us: A Collection of Discourses by Henry B. Eyring.* Salt Lake City: Deseret Book, 2002.
———. *To Draw Closer to God: A Collection of Discourses by Henry B. Eyring.* Salt Lake City: Deseret Book, 1997.
The First Vision [manual]. Salt Lake City: The Church of Jesus Christ of Latter-day Saints, 2020.
The Guide to the Scriptures. Salt Lake City: The Church of Jesus Christ of Latter-day Saints, 1993.
Hales, Robert D. "The Holy Ghost." *Ensign,* May 2016.
Hanks, Marion D. *Bread Upon the Waters.* Salt Lake City: Bookcraft, 1991.
Harper, Steven C. *First Vision: Memory and Mormon Origins.* New York: Oxford University Press, 2019.
———. *Joseph Smith's First Vision: A Guide to the Historical Accounts.* Salt Lake City: Deseret Book, 2012.
Hatch, Nathan. *The Democratization of American Christianity.* New Haven, CT: Yale University Press, 1989.
Hinckley, Gordon B. *Faith: The Essence of True Religion.* Salt Lake City: Deseret Book, 1989.
———. "Inspirational Thoughts." *Ensign,* June 2004.
———. *Teachings of Gordon B. Hinckley.* Salt Lake City: Deseret Book, 1997.
History of The Church of Jesus Christ of Latter-day Saints. Edited by B. H. Roberts. 7 vols. Salt Lake City: Deseret Book, 1957.
Holland, Jeffrey R. *Broken Things to Mend.* Salt Lake City: Deseret Book, 2008.
———. "The Message, the Meaning, and the Multitude." *Ensign,* November 2019.
———. "The Only True God and Jesus Christ Whom He Hath Sent." *Ensign,* November 2007.
———. *Trusting Jesus.* Salt Lake City: Deseret Book, 2003.
———. *Witness for His Names.* Salt Lake City: Deseret Book, 2019.
Horne, Isabella M. "Testimony of Sister M. Isabella Horne." *Woman's Exponent,* June 1910.
Hutson, James H. *The Founders on Religion: A Book of Quotations.* Princeton, NJ: Princeton University Press, 2005.
Hyde, Orson. 1842 account of the First Vision. In *A Cry from the Wilderness, a Voice from the Dust or the Earth,* josephsmithpapers.org; or churchofjesuschrist.org.
Hymns of The Church of Jesus Christ of Latter-day Saints. Salt Lake City: The Church of Jesus Christ of Latter-day Saints, 1985.
Johnson, Luke Timothy. *The Creed: What Christians Believe and Why It Matters.* New York: Doubleday, 2003.
Journal of Discourses. 26 vols. Liverpool: F. D. Richards & Sons, 1851–86.
Juvenile Instructor, 15 July 1880, 162.

Kimball, Stanley B. *Heber C. Kimball: Mormon Patriarch and Pioneer.* Urbana, IL: University of Illinois Press, 1981.

King, Arthur Henry. *Arm the Children: Faith's Response to a Violent World.* Provo, UT: Brigham Young University Studies, 1998.

Kirkham, Francis W. *A New Witness for Christ in America.* 2 vols. Salt Lake City: Zion's Printing and Publishing Company, 1951.

Latter-day Saints' Messenger and Advocate 1, no. 5 (February 1835): 79.

Lectures on Faith. Salt Lake City: Deseret Book, 1985.

Lee, Harold B. *Stand Ye in Holy Places.* Salt Lake City: Deseret Book, 1974.

Madsen, Truman G. *Eternal Man.* Salt Lake City: Deseret Book, 1966.

———. "The First Vision and Its Aftermath." The Joseph Smith Lecture Series, Lecture 1. Brigham Young University Education Week, August 1978, speeches.byu.edu.

"Manuscript History of the Church," "History, 1838–1856, volume B-1 [1 September 1834–2 November 1838]," p. 637, The Joseph Smith Papers, josephsmithpapers.org/paper-summary/history-1838-1856-volume-b-1-1-september-1834-2-november-1838/1.

Marty, Martin. *Pilgrims in Their Own Land: 500 Years of Religion in America.* Boston: Little, Brown, and Company, 1984.

Matthews, Robert J. "What Is a Religious Education?" Address to Brigham Young University Religious Education Faculty, 31 August 1989.

Maxwell, Neal A. "A Choice Seer." Brigham Young University devotional, 30 March 1986.

———. *Things As They Really Are.* Salt Lake City: Deseret Book, 1978.

———. *Whom the Lord Loveth: The Journey of Discipleship.* Salt Lake City: Deseret Book, 2003.

McConkie, Bruce R. "The Bible: A Sealed Book." Eighth Annual Church Educational System Religious Educators' Symposium, August 1984.

———. *Doctrines of the Kingdom: Sermons and Writings of Bruce R. McConkie.* Edited by Mark L. McConkie. Salt Lake City: Bookcraft, 1989.

———. "Joseph Smith: A Revealer of Christ." Brigham Young University devotional address, 3 September 1978, speeches.byu.edu.

———. "The Lord God of Joseph Smith." In *Brigham Young University Speeches of the Year, 1972.* Provo, UT: Brigham Young University Press, 1972. See also speeches.byu.edu.

———. "A New Commandment: Save Thyself and Thy Kindred!" *Ensign,* August 1976.

———. *A New Witness for the Articles of Faith.* Salt Lake City: Deseret Book, 1985.

———. "Our Relationship with the Lord." Brigham Young University devotional address, 2 March 1982, speeches.byu.edu.

———. "This Generation Shall Have My Word through You." *Ensign,* June 1980.

McConkie, Joseph Fielding. *Here We Stand.* Salt Lake City: Deseret Book, 1995.

———. *Prophets and Prophecy.* Salt Lake City: Bookcraft, 1988.

McConkie, Joseph Fielding, and Robert L. Millet. *Joseph Smith, The Choice Seer: The Prophet's Greatness as Teacher, Priesthood Leader, and Restorer.* Salt Lake City: Bookcraft, 1996.

McConkie, Mark L. *Remembering Joseph: Personal Recollections of Those Who Knew the Prophet Joseph Smith.* Salt Lake City: Deseret Book, 2003.
McKay, David O. *David O. McKay* [manual]. In *Teachings of Presidents of the Church* series. Salt Lake City: The Church of Jesus Christ of Latter-day Saints, 2003.
———. *Gospel Ideals.* Salt Lake City: Improvement Era, 1954.
———. "Unity in the Home—the Church—the Nation." *Improvement Era,* February 1954.
Millet, Robert L. *The Power of the Word: Saving Doctrines from the Book of Mormon.* Salt Lake City: Deseret Book, 1994.
———. *Precept upon Precept: Joseph Smith and the Restoration of Doctrine.* Salt Lake City: Deseret Book, 2016.
Millet, Robert L., Camille Fronk Olson, Andrew C. Skinner, and Brent L. Top. *LDS Beliefs: A Doctrinal Reference.* Salt Lake City: Deseret Book, 2011.
Moore, R. Laurance. *Religious Outsiders and the Making of Americans.* New York: Oxford University Press, 1986.
Morrison, Alexander B. *Turning from Truth: A New Look at the Great Apostasy.* Salt Lake City: Deseret Book, 2005.
Mouw, Richard J. *Talking with Mormons: An Invitation to Evangelicals.* Grand Rapids, MI: Eerdmans, 2012.
Neibaur, Alexander. 1844 account of the First Vision, josephsmithpapers.org; or churchofjesuschrist.org.
Nelson, Russell M. *Accomplishing the Impossible.* Salt Lake City: Deseret Book, 2015.
———. "Closing Remarks," *Ensign,* November 2019.
———. "Revelation for the Church, Revelation for Our Lives." *Ensign,* May 2018.
———. *Teachings of Russell M. Nelson.* Salt Lake City: Deseret Book, 2018.
Nibley, Hugh. *Since Cumorah.* 2nd ed. Vol. 7 in *The Collected Works of Hugh Nibley.* 19 vols. Salt Lake City: Deseret Book and the Foundation for Ancient Research and Mormon Studies (FARMS), 1981.
Oaks, Dallin H. "Apostasy and Restoration." *Ensign,* May 1995.
Packer, Boyd K. "The Cloven Tongues of Fire," *Ensign,* May 2000.
———. "Future Leaders." *Ensign,* May 2000.
———. "Little Children." *Ensign,* November 1986.
———. "The Only True Church." *Ensign,* November 1985.
———. *Teach Ye Diligently.* Salt Lake City: Deseret Book, 1975.
Peterson, H. Donl. "The Birth and Development of the Pearl of Great Price." In *The Pearl of Great Price,* edited by Robert L. Millet and Kent P. Jackson. Vol. 2 of *Studies in Scripture* series. 8 vols. Salt Lake City: Randall Book, 1985.
———. *The Pearl of Great Price: A History and Commentary.* Salt Lake City: Deseret Book, 1987.
Pew Religious Center. "In U.S., Decline of Christianity Continues at Rapid Pace." Report, Religion and Public Life, 17 October 2019, pewforum.org.
Pratt, Orson. 1840 account of Joseph Smith's First Vision. In "An Interesting Account of Several Remarkable Visions, and of the Late Discovery of Ancient American Records," josephsmithpapers.org/paper-summary/appendix-orson-pratt-an-interesting-account-of-several-remarkable-visions-1840; or churchofjesuschrist.org.
Pratt, Parley P. *Autobiography of Parley P. Pratt.* Salt Lake City: Deseret Book, 1979.

———. *Mormonism Unveiled: Zion's Watchman Unmasked, and Its Editor, Mr. L. R. Sunderland, Exposed: Truth Vindicated: The Devil and Priestcraft in Danger*. New York: Parley P. Pratt, 1838.

Remeni, Robert. *Joseph Smith*. New York, Penguin, 2002.

Reynolds, Noel B., ed. *Early Christians in Disarray: Contemporary LDS Perspectives on the Christian Apostasy*. Provo, Utah: Foundation for Ancient Research and Mormon Studies (FARMS), 2005.

Roberts, B. H. *Outlines of Ecclesiastical History*. Salt Lake City: George Q. Cannon & Sons, 1893.

Schaff, Philip. *The Creeds of Christendom, with a History and Critical Notes*. 3 vols. 6th ed., rev. Grand Rapids, MI: Baker Book House, 1985.

Shipps, Jan. "The Reality of the Restoration and the Restoration Ideal in the Mormon Tradition." In *The American Quest for the Primitive Church*, edited by Richard T. Hughes. Urbana, IL: University of Illinois Press, 1988.

The New Shorter Oxford English Dictionary. Edited by Lesley Brown. 2 vols. Oxford: Clarendon Press, 1993.

Smith, George Albert. *Sharing the Gospel with Others*. Compiled by Preston Nibley. Salt Lake City: Deseret News Press, 1948.

Smith, Joseph. 1832 account of the First Vision, josephsmithpapers.org; or churchofjesus christ.org.

———. 1835 account of the First Vision. Dictated to Warren Parrish, josephsmith papers.org; or churchofjesuschrist.org.

———. 1838–1839 account of the First Vision. Dictated to James Mulholland, josephsmithpapers.org; or churchofjesuschrist.org.

———. 1842 account of the First Vision. In letter to John Wentworth, josephsmith papers.org; or churchofjesuschrist.org.

———. *Joseph Smith* [manual]. In *Teachings of Presidents of the Church* series. Salt Lake City: The Church of Jesus Christ of Latter-day Saints, 2007.

———. *Personal Writings of Joseph Smith*, rev. ed. Edited by Dean C. Jessee. Salt Lake City: Deseret Book, 2002.

———. *The Words of Joseph Smith: The Contemporary Accounts of the Nauvoo Discourses of the Prophet Joseph*. Edited by Andrew F. Ehat and Lyndon W. Cook. Provo, Utah: Brigham Young University Religious Studies Center, 1980.

———. "Account of Meeting, circa 16 February 1841, as Reported by William P. McIntire," pp. [11–12], The Joseph Smith Papers, josephsmithpapers.org/paper-summary/account-of-meeting-circa-16february-1841-as-reported-by-williamp-mcintire.

———. "Account of Meeting, circa 9 March 1841, as Reported by William P. McIntire," p. [14], The Joseph Smith Papers, josephsmithpapers.org/paper-summary/account-of-meeting-circa-9march-1841-as-reported-by-williamp-mcintire/1.

———. "Discourse, [5 January 1841], as Reported by Unknown Scribe–A," p. [1], The Joseph Smith Papers, josephsmithpapers.org/paper-summary/discourse-5-january-1841-as-reported-by-unknown-scribe-a/1.

———. "Discourse, 7 April 1844, as Reported by Thomas Bullock," p. 15, The Joseph Smith Papers, josephsmithpapers.org/paper-summary/discourse-7-april-1844-as-reported-by-thomas-bullock/2.

———. "Discourse, 12 May 1844, as Reported by Thomas Bullock," The Papers of Joseph Smith, josephsmithpapers.org/paper-summary/discourse-12-may-1844-as-reported-by-thomas-bullock/2.

———. "The Elders of the Church in Kirtland, to Their Brethren Abroad." *The Evening and the Morning Star,* April 1834, 152, josephsmithpapers.org.

———. "History, 1838–1856, volume A-1 [23 December 1805–30 August 1834]." The Joseph Smith Papers, josephsmithpapers.org/paper-summary/history-1838-1856-volume-a-1-23-december-1805-30-august-1834/575.

———. "History, 1838–1856, volume B-1 [1 September 1834–2 November 1838]." The Joseph Smith Papers, josephsmithpapers.org/paper-summary/history-1838-1856-volume-b-1-1-september-1834-2-november-1838/91.

———. "History, 1838–1856, volume D-1 [1 August 1842–1 July 1843]," p. 1572, The Joseph Smith Papers, josephsmithpapers.org/paper-summary/history-1838-1856-volume-d-1-1-august-1842-1-july-1843/217.

———. "History, 1838–1856, volume E-1 [1 July 1843–30 April 1844]." The Joseph Smith Papers, josephsmithpapers.org/paper-summary/history-1838-1856-volume-e-1-1-july-1843-30-april-1844/36.

———. "Instruction, 2 April 1843, as Reported by Willard Richards," pp. [42–43], The Joseph Smith Papers, josephsmithpapers.org/paper-summary/instruction-2-april-1843-as-reported-by-willard-richards.

———. Journal, 11 June 1843, "History, 1838–1856, volume D-1 [1 August 1842–1 July 1843]," p. 1572, The Joseph Smith Papers, josephsmithpapers.org/paper-summary-history-1838-1856-volume-d-1-1-august-184201-july-1843/217.

———. Journal, 9 July 1843, in "History, 1838–1856, volume E-1 [1 July 1843–30 April 1844]," p. 1666, josephsmithpapers.org/paper-summary/history-1838-1856-volume-e-1-1-july-1843-30-april-1844/36.

———. Journal, 23 July 1843, in "History, 1838–1856, volume E-1 [1 July 1843–30 April 1844]," p. 1681, The Papers of Joseph Smith, josephsmithpapers.org/paper-summary/history-1838-1856-volume-e-1-1-july-1843-30-april-1844/51.

———. Journal, 15 October 1843, josephsmithpapers.org.

———. "Letter to Isaac Galland, 22 March 1839," p. 54, The Joseph Smith Papers, josephsmithpapers.org/paper-summary/letter-to-isaac-galland-22-march-1839/4.

———. Letter to the Church, ca. March 1834, josephsmithpapers.org/paper-summary/letter-to-the-church-circa-march-1834/3.

———. "Letter to the Elders of the Church, 30 November–1 December 1835," p. 229, The Joseph Smith Papers, josephsmithpapers.org/paper-summary/letter-to-the-elders-of-the-church-30-november-1-december-1835/5.

———. "Letter to Silas Smith, 26 September 1833," pp. 4–5, The Joseph Smith Papers, josephsmithpapers.org/paper-summary/letter-to-silas-smith-26-september-1833.

———. "Try the Spirits." *Times and Seasons* 3 (1 April 1842): 743, josephsmithpapers.org.

Smith, Joseph F. *Gospel Doctrine.* Salt Lake City: Deseret Book, 1971.

Smith, Joseph Fielding. *Answers to Gospel Questions.* 5 vols. Salt Lake City: Deseret Book, 1957–66.

———. *Doctrines of Salvation.* Compiled by Bruce R. McConkie. 3 vols. Salt Lake City: Bookcraft, 1954–56.

———. *Man: His Origin and Destiny.* Salt Lake City: Deseret Book, 1954.
Smith, Lucy Mack. *History of Joseph Smith by His Mother.* Edited by Preston Nibley. Salt Lake City: Bookcraft, n.d.
Smith, William. In interview by E. C. Briggs and J. W. Peterson. *Deseret News*, 20 January 1894.
Snow, Eliza R. *Biography and Family Record of Lorenzo Snow.* Salt Lake City: Deseret News, 1884.
The Standard of Truth. Vol. 1 of *Saints: The Story of The Church of Jesus Christ of Latter-day Saints.* 4 vols. Salt Lake City: The Church of Jesus Christ of Latter-day Saints, 2018.
Tanner, Norman P. *The Councils of the Church: A Short History.* New York: Crossroad Publishing, 2001.
Turner, J. B. *Mormonism in All Ages.* New York: Platt and Peters, 1842.
Turner, Rodney. "The Visions of Moses." In *The Pearl of Great Price,* edited by Robert L. Millet and Kent P. Jackson. Vol. 2 of *Studies in Scripture* series. 8 vols. Salt Lake City: Randall Book, 1985.
Uchtdorf, Dieter F. "You Matter to Him." *Ensign*, November 2011.
Webster, Noah. *An American Dictionary of the English Language.* 1828. Reprint, San Francisco, CA: Foundation for American Christian Education, 1985.
White, David Nye. 1843 account of the First Vision, josephsmithpapers.org; or churchofjesuschrist.org.
Whitney, Orson F. *Life of Heber C. Kimball.* 4th edition. Salt Lake City: Bookcraft, 1973.
Widtsoe, John A. *Joseph Smith—Seeker After Truth, Prophet of God.* Salt Lake City: Deseret Book, 1951.
Wilcox, Miranda, and John D. Young, eds. *Standing Apart: Mormon Historical Consciousness and the Concept of Apostasy.* New York: Oxford University Press, 2014.
Williams, Peter W. *America's Religions: From Their Origins to the Twenty-First Century.* 4th ed. Urbana, IL: University of Illinois Press, 2015.
Woodruff, Wilford. Journal, 11 June 1843, josephsmithpapers.org.

NOTES

Epigraphs (unnumbered)

McKay, *Gospel Ideals*, 85.
Benson, *God, Family, Country*, 57.
Nelson, *Accomplishing the Impossible*, 1–2.

Preface

1. *Teachings of Gordon B. Hinckley*, 226; emphasis added.
2. *Teachings of Gordon B. Hinckley*, 227.
3. *Ezra Taft Benson* [manual], 105.
4. Packer, "Little Children," *Ensign*, November 1986.

Chapter 1: How It All Began

1. See Packer, *Teach Ye Diligently*, 76–77.
2. *Clementine Recognitions*, III, 34; cited in Nibley, *Since Cumorah*, 97; emphasis added.
3. From the King Follett Sermon, 7 April 1844; see "Discourse, 7 April 1844, as Reported by Thomas Bullock," p. 15, josephsmithpapers.org; spelling and punctuation standardized. See also Ehat and Cook, *Words of Joseph Smith*, 348.
4. McConkie, *Here We Stand*, 194–95; emphasis added.
5. *Joseph Smith* [manual], 85.
6. *Guide to the Scriptures*, s.v. "Dispensation"; churchofjesuschrist.org/study/scriptures/gs/dispensation?lang=eng.
7. McConkie, "This Generation Shall Have My Word through You," *Ensign*, June 1980; see also McConkie, "Joseph Smith: A Revealer of Christ."
8. Only six weeks before his death, Joseph Smith stated: "The ancient prophets declared that in the last days the God of heaven should set up a kingdom that should never be destroyed, nor left to other people. . . . I calculate to be one of the instruments of setting up the kingdom of [God as foreseen by] Daniel by the word of the Lord, and I intend to lay a foundation that will revolutionize the whole world" (*Joseph Smith* [manual], 511–12).

9. *Joseph Smith* [manual], 510.
10. Baugh, "Joseph Smith: Seer, Translator, Revelator, and Prophet."
11. Widtsoe, *Joseph Smith*, 4.
12. See josephsmithpapers.org; or churchofjesuschrist.org.
13. "History, 1838–1856, volume B-1 [1 September 1834–2 November 1838]," p. 637; spelling modernized. See also churchofjesuschrist.org; *History of The Church of Jesus Christ of Latter-day Saints*, 2:304.
14. See josephsmithpapers.org; or churchofjesuschrist.org.
15. See josephsmithpapers.org; or churchofjesuschrist.org.

Chapter 2: The Winds of Revivalism

1. Pew Religious Center, "In U.S., Decline of Christianity Continues at Rapid Pace." According to that report, as of October 2019, 26 percent of the population of the United States has disaffiliated from any religious organization.
2. Remini, *Joseph Smith*, 4–5.
3. This expression describes the effect of the "fires" of revivalism that swept through the northeastern part of the United States.
4. Williams, *America's Religions*, 189.
5. Cartwright, *Backwoods Preacher*, 159; spelling modernized.
6. Campbell, *Christian Baptist*, 1:33.
7. Backman, *American Religions and the Rise of Mormonism*, 241.
8. Emerson, "Harvard Divinity School Address," in *Theology in America*, 306, 315.
9. See Lucy Mack Smith, *History of Joseph Smith by His Mother*, 43–53.
10. Bushman, "Visionary World of Joseph Smith," 185–86.
11. Bushman, "Visionary World of Joseph Smith," 192.
12. Bushman, "The Visionary World of Joseph Smith," 193; emphasis added.
13. Clinton, in William W. Campbell, *Life and Writings of DeWitt Clinton*, 106–7.
14. Harper, *Joseph Smith's First Vision*, 17.
15. Butler, Wacker, and Balmer, *Religion in American Life*, 217.
16. Neibaur, 1844 account, josephsmithpapers.org; or churchofjesuschrist.org.
17. Smith, 1835 account, josephsmithpapers.org; or churchofjesuschrist.org.
18. Smith, 1842 account (Wentworth letter), josephsmithpapers.org; or churchofjesuschrist.org.
19. In Orson Hyde's account of the First Vision (1842), he indicated that the boy Joseph "discovered the world of religion working under a flood of errors which by virtue of their contradictory opinions and principles laid the foundation for the rise of such different sects and denominations whose feelings toward each other all too often were poisoned by hate, contention, resentment, and anger. He felt that there was only one truth and that those who understood it correctly, all understood it in the same way" (josephsmithpapers.org; or churchofjesuschrist.org).
20. Bushman, "A Joseph Smith for the Twenty-First Century," 167; emphasis added; see also Bushman, *Believing History*, 274.
21. Backman, "Awakenings in the Burned-Over District," 307, 311.
22. Interview by Briggs and Peterson, *Deseret News*, 20 January 1894.
23. Cannon, *Life of Joseph Smith the Prophet*, 30–31.
24. Pratt, 1840 account, josephsmithpapers.org; or churchofjesuschrist.org.

25. McConkie, *New Witness for the Articles of Faith*, 5.
26. Young, in *Journal of Discourses*, 5:75.
27. Young, in *Journal of Discourses*, 8:228.
28. Woodruff, in *Journal of Discourses*, 4:100.
29. Hyde, 1842 account, josephsmithpapers.org; or churchofjesuschrist.org.
30. *Joseph Smith* [manual], 510; emphasis added.

Chapter 3: Entering the Grove

1. See *Joseph Smith* [manual], 195.
2. Enders, in *Encyclopedia of Mormonism*, 3:1247.
3. White, 1843 account, josephsmithhistory.org; emphasis added; or churchofjesuschrist.org.
4. Hales, "The Holy Ghost," *Ensign*, May 2016.
5. Eyring, *Because He First Loved Us*, 58–59; emphasis added.
6. Harper, *Joseph Smith's First Vision*, 89. See also Eyring, *To Draw Closer to God*, 35–36.
7. Andersen, *Divine Gift of Forgiveness*, 110.
8. "There is a lesson in the Prophet Joseph Smith's account of the First Vision which virtually every Latter-day Saint has had occasion to experience, or one day soon will. It is the plain and very sobering truth that before great moments, certainly before great spiritual moments, there can come adversity, opposition, and darkness. Life has some of those moments for us, and occasionally they come just as we are approaching an important decision or a significant step in our lives" (Holland, *Trusting Jesus*, 167).
9. In his 1844 account, Alexander Neibaur explained that Joseph "went into the woods to pray [and] knelt himself down. His tongue cleaved to his roof [the roof of his mouth]. He could utter not a word. He felt easier after a while" (josephsmithpapers.org; or churchofjesuschrist.org).
10. *The First Vision* [manual], "Journal, 9–11 November 1835."
11. Hyde, 1842 account, josephsmithpapers.org; emphasis added; or churchofjesuschrist.org.
12. See *Lectures on Faith*, 42, 52–53, 54, 71.
13. Hanks, *Bread Upon the Waters*, 257; emphasis added.
14. Whitney, *Life of Heber C. Kimball*, 131–32; see also Kimball, *Heber C. Kimball*, 47–48.

Chapter 4: The Appearance

1. Millet, Olson, Skinner, and Top, *LDS Beliefs*, 632.
2. Nelson, *Teachings of Russell M. Nelson*, 166–67.
3. "Discourse, 12 May 1844, as Reported by Thomas Bullock," josephsmithpapers.org; see also Smith, *Words of Joseph Smith*, 368.
4. Pratt, "An Interesting Account of Several Remarkable Visions, 1840," p. 5, josephsmithpapers.org; emphasis added. See also Pratt, in *Journal of Discourses*, 14:141, 17:279.
5. *The First Vision* [manual], "Journal, 9–11 November 1835; emphasis added."
6. Smith, 1835 account, josephsmithpapers.org; emphasis added; or churchofjesuschrist.org; White, 1843 account, josephsmithpapers.org; or churchofjesuschrist.org.
7. This is the position taken in *Standard of Truth*, 15–16.

8. *Joseph Smith* [manual], 42.
9. White, 1843 account, and Smith, 1835 account, josephsmithpapers.org; emphasis added; or churchofjesuschrist.org.
10. Smith, 1832 account, josephsmithpapers.org; emphasis added; or churchofjesuschrist.org.
11. Taylor, in *Journal of Discourses*, 21:65; emphasis added.
12. See Webster, *American Dictionary of the English Language* (1828), s.v. "Lord."
13. McConkie, *Doctrines of the Kingdom*, 64.
14. Smith, 1842 account (Wentworth letter); Pratt, 1840 account; Hyde, 1842 account; and Neibaur, 1844 account; josephsmithpapers.org; emphasis added; or churchofjesuschrist.org.
15. Backman, *Joseph Smith's First Vision*, 201–2. In fact, Matthew B. Christensen has demonstrated just how beautiful and inspiring a harmonization of the various accounts really is (*First Vision*).
16. Anderson, "Parallel Prophets: Paul and Joseph Smith," 178–79.
17. Harper, *First Vision*, 40–41.
18. Harper, *Joseph Smith's First Vision*, 80–81; emphasis added.
19. Smith, *Doctrines of Salvation*, 1:27.
20. Smith, *Man: His Origin and Destiny,* 304; see also Smith, *Answers to Gospel Questions*, 3:38.
21. Widtsoe, *Joseph Smith—Seeker After Truth,* 4.
22. Smith, *Doctrines of Salvation,* 1:28; see also Smith, *Answers to Gospel Questions*, 1:16–17.
23. Smith, 1835 account, josephsmithpapers.org; emphasis added; or churchofjesuschrist.org.
24. Harper, *Joseph Smith's First Vision*, 91.
25. Madsen, "First Vision and Its Aftermath."
26. Pratt, in *Journal of Discourses,* 14:140.
27. Holland, "The Message, the Meaning, and the Multitude," *Ensign,* November 2019; emphasis added.
28. *Teachings of Gordon B. Hinckley*, 225.

Chapter 5: "Their Hearts Are Far from Me"

1. Smith, 1842 account (Wentworth letter), josephsmithpapers.org; or churchofjesuschrist.org.
2. Smith, 1838 account, Joseph Smith–History, 1:16–17; "Try the Spirits," *Times and Seasons,* 1 April 1842, josephsmithpapers.org.
3. Asay, "'Oh, How Lovely Was the Morning!': Joseph Smith's First Prayer and the First Vision," *Ensign*, April 1995.
4. Smith, 1832 account, josephsmithpapers.org; emphasis added; or churchofjesuschrist.org.
5. Smith, 1835 account, josephsmithpapers.org; emphasis added; or churchofjesuschrist.org.
6. Bednar, "Ask in Faith," *Ensign,* May 2008; emphasis added.
7. Smith, 1832 account, josephsmithpapers.org; or churchofjesuschrist.org.
8. The Prophet Joseph's language in the Wentworth letter (1842) was softer than

the Lord's but still direct and to the point: "They [the Father and the Son] told me that all religious denominations were believing in incorrect doctrines, and that none of them was acknowledged of God as his church and kingdom. And I was expressly commanded to 'go not after them'" (josephsmithpapers.org; or churchofjesuschrist.org).
9. McKay, "Unity in the Home—the Church—the Nation," *Improvement Era*, February 1954, 77.
10. Joseph Smith, Journal, 11 June 1843, in "History, 1838–1856, volume D-1 [1 August 1842–1 July 1843]," p. 1572, josephsmithpapers.org. See also Wilford Woodruff, Journal, 11 June 1843, josephsmithpapers.org.
11. Pratt, in *Journal of Discourses*, 7:28; emphasis added.
12. *Joseph Smith* [manual], 207.
13. Smith, "Letter to the Elders of the Church, 30 November–1 December 1835," p. 229, josephsmithpapers.org.
14. Maxwell, *Whom the Lord Loveth*, 129.
15. *Joseph Smith* [manual], 93.
16. *Joseph Smith* [manual], 41–42.
17. Oaks, "Apostasy and Restoration," *Ensign*, May 1995; see also Holland, *Broken Things to Mend*, 151–52.
18. Durant, *Caesar and Christ*, 595, in Cook, "Valiant in the Testimony of Jesus," *Ensign*, November 2016; emphasis added.
19. Other books on the Great Apostasy written by members of The Church of Jesus Christ of Latter-day Saints include Reynolds, *Early Christians in Disarray*; Callister, *Inevitable Apostasy*; Wilcox and Young, *Standing Apart*.
20. Morrison, *Turning from Truth*, 52; see also Boyd K. Packer, "The Cloven Tongues of Fire," *Ensign*, May 2000.
21. Joseph Smith, Journal, 9 July 1843, in "History, 1838–1856, volume E-1 [1 July 1843–30 April 1844]," p. 1666, josephsmithpapers.org.
22. Joseph Smith, Journal, 23 July 1843, in "History, 1838–1856, volume E-1 [1 July 1843–30 April 1844]," p. 1681, josephsmithpapers.org.
23. Smith, *Sharing the Gospel with Others*, 12–13; emphasis added.
24. See also Joseph Smith History, in History, 1838–1856, volume A-1 [23 December 1805–30 August 1834], 183]; Letter to the Church, ca. March 1834; Joseph Smith, Journal, 15 October 1843; Joseph Smith History, vol. E-1, 1754–1755, josephsmithpapers.org; see also Smith, *Words of Joseph Smith*, 256.
25. McConkie, *Doctrines of the Kingdom*, 280; or churchofjesuschrist.org/study/manual/teaching-seminary-preservice-readings-religion-370-471-and-475/the-bible-a-sealed-book.
26. See Ballard, "The Miracle of the Holy Bible," *Ensign*, May 2007.
27. Whitney, in Conference Report, April 1928, 59, quoted in Benson, "Civic Standards for the Faithful Saints," *Ensign*, July 1972.
28. Benson, "Born of God," *Ensign*, November 1985.
29. Maxwell, *Things As They Really Are*, 45; emphasis added.
30. See Joseph Fielding McConkie, *Prophets and Prophecy*, 174–75; see also Webster, *American Dictionary of the English Language* (1828), s.v. "true"; *The New Shorter Oxford English Dictionary*, s.v., "true"; Ayto, *Word Origins*, s.v. "true."

31. Maxwell, *Things as They Really Are*, 46.
32. Balmer, *Mine Eyes Have Seen the Glory*, 24.
33. See also Packer, "The Only True Church," *Ensign*, November 1985.
34. Hinckley, "Inspirational Thoughts," *Ensign*, June 2004; emphasis added.

Chapter 6: "All Their Creeds"

1. In relating the Lord's words to Joseph Smith, Elder Orson Pratt said, "He was immediately told, that there was no true church of Christ on the earth, that all had gone astray, and *had framed doctrines, and dogmas, and creeds by human wisdom*, and that the authority to administer in the holy ordinances of the Gospel was not among men upon the earth" (in *Journal of Discourses*, 17:279; emphasis added).
2. McConkie, *Lord God of Joseph Smith*, 4; emphasis added.
3. To learn more about the Christian creeds, see Schaff, *Creeds of Christendom*; Tanner, *Councils of the Church*; and Johnson, *The Creed*.
4. *Joseph Smith* [manual], 39–40; emphasis added.
5. Turner, "Visions of Moses," 45; emphasis added.
6. Adams Diary, 18 February 1756, in Hutson, *Founders on Religion*, 79; spelling and punctuation modernized.
7. Abigail Adams to Louisa Catherine Adams, 3 January 1818, in Hutson, *Founders on Religion*, 79; spelling and punctuation modernized.
8. Thomas Jefferson to Thomas Whittemore, 5 June 1822, in Hutson, *Founders on Religion*, 81; spelling and punctuation modernized.
9. See Oaks, "Apostasy and Restoration," *Ensign*, May 1995; see also page 64 herein.
10. "History, 1838–1856, volume B-1 [1 September 1834–2 November 1838]," p. 794, josephsmithpapers.org; spelling and capitalization modernized; see also Doctrine and Covenants 123:7–8 (March 1839); *History of the Church*, 2:271 (March 1839); 3:28 (May 1838).
11. Letter to Isaac Galland, 22 March 1839, in Jessee, *Personal Writings of Joseph Smith*, 457–58; see "Letter to Isaac Galland, 22 March 1839," josephsmithpapers.org. See also Smith, "Try the Spirits," *Times and Seasons* 3, no. 11 (1 April 1842): 743, josephsmithpapers.org.
12. *Joseph Smith* [manual], 264.
13. Bangerter, "It's a Two-Way Street," 161–62, speeches.byu.edu; emphasis added.
14. Asay, "'Oh, How Lovely Was the Morning!': Joseph Smith's First Prayer and the First Vision," *Ensign*, April 1995.
15. Joseph Smith, Journal, 15 October 1843; Joseph Smith History, October 1843, in "History, 1838–1856, volume E-1 [1 July 1843–30 April 1844]," pp. 1754–55, josephsmithpapers.org; emphasis added.
16. *Teachings of Gordon B. Hinckley*, 236.

Chapter 7: After the Vision

1. White, 1843 account, and Neibaur, 1844 account, josephsmithpapers.org; or churchofjesuschrist.org.
2. Joseph Smith History, Draft Notes, 14 March 1843, in "History, 1838–1856, volume D-1 [1 August 1842–1 July 1843]," p. 1497, josephsmithpapers.org; emphasis added.

3. Madsen, "First Vision and Its Aftermath."
4. In Andrus and Andrus, *They Knew the Prophet*, 68; see also Mark L. McConkie, *Remembering Joseph*, 252–53.
5. See *The 1647 Westminster Confession of Faith*, chapter 2: "Of God, and of the Holy Trinity"; apuritansmind.com/westminster-standards/chapter-2/; emphasis added.
6. See Lucy Mack Smith, *History of Joseph Smith by His Mother*.
7. Smith, 1835 and 1832 accounts, respectively, josephsmithpapers.org; emphasis added; or churchofjesuschrist.org.
8. Snow, *Biography and Family Record of Lorenzo Snow*, 7–8; emphasis added.
9. Smith, 1842 account (Wentworth letter), josephsmithpapers.org; or churchofjesuschrist.org.
10. Orson Pratt, in *Journal of Discourses*, 12:355.
11. Smith, 1832 account, josephsmithpapers.org; or churchofjesuschrist.org.
12. Pratt, in *Journal of Discourses*, 17:279–80; emphasis added.
13. Horne, "Testimony of Sister M. Isabella Horne," 6.
14. Pratt, in *Journal of Discourses*, 17:280.
15. *Standard of Truth*, 17.
16. Neibaur, 1844 account, and White, 1843 account, josephsmithpapers.org; or churchofjesuschrist.org. On 11 June 1843 Levi Richards attended a lecture delivered by the Prophet in which Joseph made some remarks about his First Vision. Richards's diary contains a very brief entry that includes the following: "Earth and hell had opposed him and tried to destroy him, but they had not done it and never would" (in Allen and Welch, "Appearance of the Father and the Son to Joseph Smith in 1820," in *Exploring the First Vision*, 57).
17. Pratt, in *Journal of Discourses*, 17:280–81; emphasis added.
18. Moore, *Religious Outsiders and the Making of Americans*, xiii.
19. Shipps, "Reality of the Restoration and the Restoration Ideal," 182–83; emphasis in original.
20. Mouw, *Talking with Mormons*, 62–63; emphasis added.
21. Allen, "Emergence of a Fundamental," 51–53.
22. Allen, "Emergence of a Fundamental," 51–53.
23. Allen, "Emergence of a Fundamental," 54; see Cannon, "Editorial Thoughts," *Juvenile Instructor*, 15 July 1880, 162; see also Cannon, in *Journal of Discourses*, 24:371–72. In 1893 Elder B. H. Roberts pointed out that Joseph Smith's First Vision was particularly significant because "it revealed that [God] had both body and parts, that he was in the form of man, or, rather, that man had been made in [God's] image" (*Outlines of Ecclesiastical History*, 299).
24. In Peterson, "Birth and Development of the Pearl of Great Price," 11–12; see also Peterson, *Pearl of Great Price*, 6–24.
25. See "Oh Say, What Is Truth?" *Hymns*, no. 272.
26. McConkie, "A New Commandment: Save Thyself and Thy Kindred!" *Ensign*, August 1976.
27. *Joseph Smith* [manual], 520.
28. *Teachings of Russell M. Nelson*, 170; emphasis added.

Chapter 8: What Joseph Learned

1. Cannon, *Life of Joseph Smith the Prophet*, 32, referring to John 17:3.
2. Smith, 1832 account, josephsmithpapers.org; or churchofjesuschrist.org.
3. Asay, "'Oh, How Lovely Was the Morning!': Joseph Smith's First Prayer and the First Vision," *Ensign*, April 1995; paragraphing altered.
4. McConkie, *Here We Stand*, 194.
5. Nelson, "Revelation for the Church, Revelation for Our Lives," *Ensign*, May 2018; emphasis added. See also Doctrine and Covenants 42:61.
6. Pratt, 1840 account, josephsmithpapers.org; or churchofjesuschrist.org.
7. Hyde, 1842 account, josephsmithpapers.org; emphasis added; or churchofjesuschrist.org.
8. Eyring, in Andersen, *Divine Gift of Forgiveness*, 177–78; emphasis added.
9. Smith, *Words of Joseph Smith*, 60. See also "Discourse, [5 January 1841], as Reported by Unknown Scribe–A," p. [1], josephsmithpapers.org.
10. Smith, *Words of Joseph Smith*, 63. See also "Account of Meeting, circa 16 February 1841, as Reported by William P. McIntire," pp. [11–12], josephsmithpapers.org.
11. Smith, *Words of Joseph Smith*, 64. See also "Account of Meeting, circa 9 March 1841, as Reported by William P. McIntire," p. [14], josephsmithpapers.org.
12. Smith, *Words of Joseph Smith*, 173. See also "Instruction, 2 April 1843, as Reported by Willard Richards," pp. [42–43], josephsmithpapers.org.
13. Backman, "Truman Coe's 1836 Description of Mormonism," 354; emphasis added.
14. Holland, *Witness for His Names*, 106.
15. *Joseph Smith* [manual], 41–42.
16. Elder Carlos E. Asay of the Seventy stated: "Joseph learned with one glance and through few spoken words the true doctrine of the oneness of the Godhead—a doctrine that had been confused for centuries by misguided men. There appeared before him two personages who were as separate and distinct as any earthly father and son. Yet, the two personages displayed a perfect unity of mind and purpose that could not be refuted. The Father expressed his love for the Son and invited him to speak, knowing that the Son would say what the Father would say if he had chosen to be voice" ("'Oh, How Lovely Was the Morning!': Joseph Smith's First Prayer and the First Vision," *Ensign*, April 1995).
17. *Lectures on Faith*, 60.
18. Holland, "The Only True God and Jesus Christ Whom He Hath Sent," *Ensign*, November 2007.
19. See Joseph Fielding Smith, *Doctrines of Salvation*, 1:27.
20. Smith, 1842 account (Wentworth letter); josephsmithpapers.org; emphasis added; or churchofjesuschrist.org.
21. Smith, "Letter to Isaac Galland," in Jessee, *Personal Writings of Joseph Smith*, 322–24; spelling and punctuation modernized. See also "Letter to Silas Smith, 26 September 1833," pp. 4–5, josephsmithpapers.org.
22. Roberts, in Harper, *First Vision*, 155.
23. Maxwell, *Whom the Lord Loveth*, 132; paragraphing altered.
24. Uchtdorf, "You Matter to Him," *Ensign*, November 2011; paragraphing altered.

25. Nelson, "Closing Remarks," *Ensign*, November 2019; emphasis added; paragraphing altered.

Chapter 9: Formative and Foundational to Our Faith

1. Widtsoe, *Joseph Smith*, 8–9; emphasis added.
2. McKay, *David O. McKay* [manual], 93.
3. Bushman, "What Can We Learn from the First Vision?" in Harper, *First Vision*, 250–52; emphasis added.
4. Hinckley, *Faith: The Essence of True Religion*, 9–10.
5. Pratt, *Autobiography of Parley P. Pratt*, 298.
6. *Autobiography of Parley P. Pratt*, 299.
7. A humorous but instructive account of an experience of Elder Matthew Cowley emphasizes the peace and power that flow from an expression of loyalty toward Joseph Smith and the Restoration. "I was called on a mission," Brother Cowley began. "And I will never forget the prayers of my father the day that I left. I have never heard a more beautiful blessing in all my life. Then his last words to me at the railroad station, 'My boy, you will go out on that mission; you will study; you will try to prepare your sermons; and sometimes when you are called upon, you will think you are wonderfully prepared, but when you stand up, your mind will go completely blank.' I have had that experience more than once." Brother Cowley then asked what he should do in such instances. His father replied, "'You stand up there and with all the fervor of your soul, you bear witness that Joseph Smith was a prophet of the living God, and thoughts will flood into your mind and words to your mouth, to round out those thoughts in a facility of expression that will carry conviction to the heart of everyone who listens.' And so my mind, being mostly blank during my five years in the mission field, gave me the opportunity to bear testimony to the greatest event in the history of the world since the crucifixion of the Master. Try it some time, fellows and girls. If you don't have anything else to say, testify that Joseph Smith was the prophet of God, and the whole history of the Church will flood into your mind, . . . if you will but bear testimony that the prophet was indeed a servant of God and an instrument in his hands" (*Matthew Cowley Speaks*, 297–98).
8. Lee, *Stand Ye in Holy Places*, 92.
9. King, *Arm the Children*, 42–43.
10. McConkie, *Here We Stand*, 195.
11. Clark, "Charted Course of the Church in Education."
12. Clark, "Charted Course of the Church in Education."
13. Clark, "Charted Course of the Church in Education"; emphasis added.

INDEX

Abomination, 75
Acting upon knowledge, 58–59
Adams, Abigail, 77
Adams, John, 77
Age of Enlightenment, 11
Allen, James B., 93
Andersen, Neil L., 34
Anderson, Richard Lloyd, 49–50
Angels, 53
Anti-Mormon literature, 119
Apostasy, 59, 60–65, 98–99, 152–53n8, 154n1
Apostolic priesthood authority, 66
Articles of Faith, 95
Asay, Carlos E., 80, 99, 156n16
Asking in faith, 58–59

Backman, Milton V. Jr., 22–23, 49, 106
Balmer, Randall, 71–72
Bangerter, W. Grant, 78–79
Baptism, 69
Barstow, George, 9
Baugh, Alex, 7
Bednar, David A., 58–59
Benson, Ezra Taft, v, x, 68
Bible: Revivalist interpretations of, 22; James 1:5, 23–24, 31, 99–101; Joseph's realization concerning, 33; inconsistency of accounts in, 47–51; plain and precious truths lost from, 62, 67–68; interpretation of, 71–72, 99; teachings on eternal marriage in, 116–18
Biblical sufficiency, 89–90
Blood, woman with issue of, 85
Body, of God, 104–5, 155n23
Bushman, Richard L., 16, 17, 22, 114–15

Campbell, Alexander, 14, 15
Cannon, George Q., 23, 93, 95, 98
Cartwright, Peter, 14
Celestial kingdom, 69
Cessationism, 90–91
Chamberlain, Solomon, 16–17
Christian church councils, 75–76
Christianity: apostasy in, 59, 60–65, 98–99, 152–53n8, 154n1; truth in churches of, 66–68; salvation in, 68–69
Christian Primitivism, 14–15
Christians: persecution of early, 60–61; infighting among early, 61; sincerity of, 66–68; salvation of, 68–69; hypocritical behavior of, 79–80
Church councils, 75–76
Church of Jesus Christ of Latter-day Saints, The: First Vision as founding event of, ix, 113–14; as "only true

church," 65–73; opposition to, 91–92; growth of, 94
Clark, J. Reuben Jr., 124–26
Clayton, William, 105
Clement of Rome, 4
Clinton, DeWitt, 17–18
Coe, Truman, 106
Commandments of men, 80–81
Contention, 99
Continuing revelation, 108–9
Conversion, 122
Cook, Quentin L., 64
Cowley, Matthew, 157n7
Creeds/Creedalism, 74–78, 80–81, 82

Degrees of glory, 69
Deification, 76
Dibble, Philo, 86
Dispensation of the fulness of times, 6
Dispensations, 5–6
Doctrine: order in teaching, 3–4; contested, during time of religious tumult, 20–23; apostasy and loss of, 61–65; creedalism's confusion of, 77; revealed during Restoration, 111–12
Durant, Will, 64

Edwards, Jonathan, 11–12
Emerson, Ralph Waldo, 14–15
Enders, Donald L., 30
Eternal marriage, 116–17
Eyring, Henry B., 32, 104

Faith: asking in, 58–59; crises of, 114–15, 119–22
Finney, Charles Grandison, 12–13
First Great Awakening, 11–12
First Vision: faith in, ix–x; as founding event of The Church of Jesus Christ of Latter-day Saints, ix; significance of, x, 10, 52, 113–14, 115–16, 155n23; author teaches, as missionary, 3–4; as starting point in gospel learning, 4–5; accounts of, 8–10, 47–51; Alexander Neibaur's 1844 account of, 9, 19, 45, 84–85, 91, 139, 151n9; David Nye White's 1843 account of, 9, 31, 42–43, 84, 91, 138–39; Orson Hyde's 1842 account of, 9, 24–25, 36, 103, 136–37, 150n19; Levi Richards's account of, 9, 155n16; and James 1:5's influence on Joseph Smith, 23–24, 31–32; and location of Sacred Grove, 30–31; and Joseph's reasons for entering Sacred Grove, 31–34, 56; Joseph's battle with Satan preceding, 34–37; appearance of God and Jesus Christ to Joseph Smith at, 42–45; clarifications made to accounts of, 46–47; God testifies of Jesus Christ at, 51–53; testimony of, 54; Joseph asks question during, 56–58; Joseph receives answer to question during, 58–60; Joseph weakened by, 84–86; joy experienced by Joseph following, 87–88; revelations given at, 88–89; persecution of Joseph Smith following, 89–93; Joseph hesitates to speak of, 92–93; canonization of account of, 95–96; lessons learned from, 98–112, 155n23, 156n16; information not given at, 111–12; purpose of, 115; power in Joseph Smith's testimony of, 119–26; teaching reality of, 125; author's first talk on, 126–27; Joseph's 1832 account of, 129–31; Joseph's 1835 account of, 131–32; Joseph's 1838 account of, 132–34; Orson Pratt's 1840 account of, 134–36, 154n1; Joseph's 1842 account of, 138, 152–53n8
Forgiveness, 57–58, 104

Glory, of God and Jesus Christ, 41–42
God: presence of, 40–41, 85–86; glory of, 41–42; role of the Father in Godhead, 42; appears to Joseph Smith, 42–45; as "Lord," 43–45; physical description of, 45; testifies of Jesus Christ, 51–53; calls prophets

by name, 57; nature of, 63, 76, 81, 104–5; becoming like, 76; denying power of, 81–82; restored truths regarding, 82–83, 109; as embodiment of love, 87–88; hears and answers prayers, 99–101; power of, 102–3; corporeality of, 104–5, 155n23; as united with Jesus Christ, 107–8; knows us by name, 109–10; worshipping, 114. *See also* First Vision; Godhead

Godhead: roles of members of, 42; relationship among members of, 63–64, 107–8, 156n16; creedal statement on, 75; natures of members of, 105; restored truths regarding, 109. *See also* God; Holy Ghost; Jesus Christ

Golgotha, 30

Gospel, teaching, 124–26

Gospel dispensations, 5–6

Great Britain, Church growth and publications in, 94–95

Greek philosophy, 63, 64

Hales, Robert D., 31

Hanks, Marion D., 36–37

Harper, Steven C., 33, 50–51

Hinckley, Gordon B., x, 54, 72–73, 82–83, 115–16

Holland, Jeffrey R., 53–54, 106–7, 107–8

Holy Ghost: as central to Restoration, 31; role of, in Godhead, 42; receiving confirmation through, 121, 122. *See also* Godhead

Holy Land, as sacred space, 28–29

Horne, Mary Isabella Hales, 89

Hyde, Orson: account of First Vision, 9, 36, 45, 103, 136–37, 150n19; on Joseph Smith's search for truth, 24–25; attacked by evil spirits, 38–39

Hypocrisy, 79–80

James 1:5, 23–24, 31–32, 99–101

Jefferson, Thomas, 77

Jesus Christ: Satan's confrontation of, 38; glory of, 41–42; role of, in Godhead, 42; appears to Joseph Smith, 42–45; as "Lord," 43–45; physical description of, 45; revelation through, 51, 52, 108; God testifies of, 51–53; Joseph asks question of, 56–58; answers Joseph's question, 58–60; and woman with issue of blood, 85; as embodiment of love, 87–88; postmortal ministry of, 102; as resurrected, living being, 103; salvation through, 103–4; as united with God, 107–8; knows us by name, 109–10; worshipping, 114; faith in, 114–15; Joseph as special witness of, 114–15; teaching reality of, 125. *See also* First Vision; Godhead

Joseph Smith Building (BYU), 103–4

"Joseph Smith's First Prayer," 36–37

Joy, following First Vision, 87–88

Kimball, Heber C., 38–39

King, Arthur Henry, 123

Kingdom of God, 149n8

Kingdom of the Cults (Martin), 119

Knowledge, acting upon, 58–59

Lee, Harold B., 122

Little, James A., 93

Living, 70–71

Lord, 43–45

Louisiana meetinghouse, as sacred space, 27–28

Love, God and Jesus Christ as embodiment of, 87–88

Lucifer. *See* Satan

Madsen, Truman G., 53, 85–86

Marriage, eternal, 116–18

Marsh, Thomas B., 124

Martin, Walter, 119

Matthias / Matthews, Robert, 8

Maxwell, Neal A., 62–63, 70–71, 110

McConkie, Bruce R., 5–6, 23, 45, 67–68, 75, 96

McConkie, Joseph Fielding, 5, 100, 124
McKay, David O., v, 60–61, 113
Meetinghouse, as sacred space, 27–28
Methodism, 18–19
Millet, Anatole J., 126
Mind visions, 7
Ministers, corruption of Revivalist, 78–83
Moore, R. Laurence, 92
Mormon, Waters of, 26–27
Morrison, Alexander B., 65
Moses: Satan's confrontation of, 37–38; transfiguration of, 40
Mount of Beatitudes, 30
Mouw, Richard J., 92
Mulholland, James, 8

Name: prophets called by, 57; God and Jesus Christ know us by, 109–10
Neibaur, Alexander, account of First Vision, 9, 19, 45, 84–85, 91, 139, 151n9
Nelson, Russell M., v, 96–97, 100–101, 110–11
Nephi, 101–2
New and everlasting covenant, 63
New Measures Revivalism, 13
New York City, author's missionary work in, 1–4

Oaks, Dallin H., 64, 77
"Only true church," meaning of, 65–73
Opposition: to The Church of Jesus Christ of Latter-day Saints, 91–92; before spiritual moments, 151nn8–9. *See also* Persecution
Order, in teaching doctrine, 3–4
Ordinances, alterations to, 61–62
Others, treatment of, 79–80

Packer, Boyd K., xi, 4
Pearl of Great Price, 94–95
Persecution: of early Christians, 60–61; of Joseph Smith, 79, 89–93. *See also* Opposition
Personal visitations, 7

Peter, 4
Philadelphia, Joseph Smith's sermon in, 118–19
Pondering, 23–24, 31–32, 101–2
Pratt, Orson: account of First Vision, 9, 23, 33, 35–36, 42, 45, 102–3, 134–36, 154n1; on education of Joseph Smith, 53; on biblical corruption, 62; on persecution following First Vision, 89, 91; on biblical sufficiency, 89–90; on spiritual neediness of British Saints, 94; and Pearl of Great Price, 95
Pratt, Parley P., 15, 93, 118–19
Prayer: vocal, 34; God hears and answers, 99–101
Presbyterianism, 86
Priesthood authority, 66
Prophet(s): following, ix–x; purpose of, 5; Joseph Smith foreordained as, 6, 96; restoration of office of, 92

Question(s): answering, 3–4; of Joseph Smith at First Vision, 56–60

Reformation, 71–72, 89–90
Remini, Robert, 12
Restoration: purpose of, 83; beginning of, 108, 111; doctrine to be revealed during, 111–12; First Vision as foundation of, 113–14; loyalty to, 115–19, 157n7; author's first talk on, 126–28; and latter-day building of kingdom of God, 149n8
Restorationism, 14–15
Resurrection, 103
Revelation: through Jesus Christ, 51, 52, 108; and cessationism, 89–91; asking for, 100–101; continuing, 108–9, 117–18
Revivalism: and First Great Awakening, 11–12; and Second Great Awakening, 12–14; and Christian Primitivism, 14–15; visionary culture of, 15–17, 90; tumult of, 17–20, 53–54, 150n19; contested doctrines

of, 20–23; corruption of teachers
during, 78–83
Richards, Franklin D., 93, 94–95
Richards, Levi, 9, 155n16
Rigdon, Sidney, 15, 86, 118
Robert, B. H., 109, 155n23
Romanticism, 12

Sacred Grove: location of, 30–31;
Joseph's reasons for entering, 31–34,
56
Sacred spaces, 26–29
Salvation, 68–69, 103–4
Satan: Joseph's battle with, 34–37,
103; attempts to thwart spiritually
significant events, 37–39; contention
as tool of, 99; reality of, 102; God's
power exceeds that of, 102–3
Scriptures: pondering, 23–24, 31–32,
101–2; *Sola scriptura*, 71–72. *See also*
Bible
Second Great Awakening, 12–14
Seers, 7
Shipps, Jan, 92
Smith, Asael, 18
Smith, George Albert, 67
Smith, Hyrum, 18
Smith, Joseph Fielding, 51, 52
Smith, Joseph Jr.: on prophets, 5; on
starting right, 5; as foreordained
prophet, 6, 96; pre-Restoration
religious beliefs of, 18–19; on
beginning of Restoration, 25;
reasons for entering Sacred Grove,
31–34, 56; concern of, for soul,
32–33; Satan's attack on, 34–39,
103; on Satan's attack on Orson
Hyde and Heber C. Kimball, 38–39;
transfiguration of, 40–41, 85–86;
God and Jesus Christ appear to, 42–
45; and clarifications made to First
Vision accounts, 46–47; education
of, 53; spiritual education of, 54–55,
105; God calls, by name, 57; receives
forgiveness, 57–58, 104; on biblical
corruption, 62, 63; on nature of
Godhead, 64; on truth, 67; on
character of God, 76; on creeds, 78;
persecution of, 79, 89–93; weakened
by First Vision, 84–86; recounts
First Vision to mother, 86–87; joy
of, following First Vision, 87–88;
as hesitant to speak about First
Vision, 92–93; loneliness of, 96; on
revelation, 108–9; reverence for, 114;
as special witness of Jesus Christ,
114–15; bearing testimony of, 116–
19, 157n7; speaks in Philadelphia,
118–19; power in testimony of,
119–26; 1832 account of First
Vision, 129–31; 1835 account of
First Vision, 131–32; 1838 account
of First Vision, 132–34; 1840
account of First Vision, 134–36;
1842 account of First Vision, 138,
152–53n8; on setting up of kingdom
of God, 149n8; searches for truth,
150n19. *See also* First Vision
Smith, Joseph Sr., 18
Smith, Lucy Mack, 18, 86–87
Smith, Samuel Harrison, 18
Smith, Sophronia, 18
Smith, William, 23
Snow, Lorenzo, 87
Sola scriptura, 71–72
Soul: Joseph Smith's concern for, 32–33;
reality of immortality of, 103
Spiritual experiences: weakness from,
84–86; joy following, 87; darkness
before, 151nn8–9
Spirit world, Joseph F. Smith's vision of,
102
Stearns, Norris, 17
Street meeting, in New York City, 1–4

Taylor, John, 44
Teaching, order in, 3–4
Testimony: of First Vision, 54, 115–19,
157n7; power in Joseph Smith's,
119–26; of author, 126–28
Theophany, 6
Theosis, 4

Transfiguration, 40–41, 85–86
Treatment of others, 79–80
True, 70
Truth: in Christian churches, 65–68; Joseph Smith on creeds and embracing, 78; Joseph Smith's search for, 150n19
Turner, Rodney, 76

Uchtdorf, Dieter F., 110
Unity, of Godhead, 107–8, 156n16
Universalism, 18

Vision: given to Nephi, 101–2; given to Joseph F. Smith, 102
Visionary culture, 15–17, 90
Visions, 6–8

Wacker, Grant, 18
Waters of Mormon, 26–27
Weakness, from spiritual experiences, 84–86
Wentworth, John, 9
Wentworth Letter, 9, 20, 41–42, 45, 56, 88, 138, 152–53n8
Wesley, John, 12, 18–19
White, David Nye, account of First Vision, 9, 31, 42–43, 84, 91, 138–39
Whitefield, George, 12
Whitney, Orson F., 68
Widtsoe, John A., 7–8, 52, 113
Woman with issue of blood, 85
Worship, for God and Jesus Christ, 114

Young, Brigham, 24